Manager's Guide to Crisis Management

To learn more about titles in the Briefcase Books series go to
www.briefcasebooks.com

Manager's Guide to Crisis Management

Jonathan Bernstein
with Bruce Bonafede

McGraw-Hill

New York Chicago San Francisco Lisbon
London Madrid Mexico City Milan New Delhi
San Juan Seoul Singapore Sydney Toronto

The McGraw·Hill Companies

1 2 3 4 5 6 7 8 9 0 QFR/QFR 6 5 4 3 2 1

ISBN   978-0-07-176949-5
MHID   0-07-176949-8

e-ISBN   978-0-07-177613-3
e-MHID   0-07-177613-4

This is a CWL Publishing Enterprises book developed for McGraw-Hill by CWL Publishing Enterprises, Inc., Madison, Wisconsin, www.cwlpub.com.

Library of Congress Cataloging-in-Publication Data

Bernstein, Jonathan (Jonathan L.)
   Manager's guide to crisis management / by Jonathan Bernstein.
      p. cm.
   Includes index.
   ISBN-13: 978-0-07-176949-5 (alk. paper)
   ISBN-10: 0-07-176949-8 (alk. paper)
   1. Crisis management. I. Title.
HD49.B475 2012
658.4'056—dc23   2011034263

Product or brand names used in this book may be trade names or trademarks. Where we believe there may be proprietary claims to such trade names or trademarks, the name has been used with an initial capital or it has been capitalized in the style used by the name claimant. Regardless of the capitalization used, all such names have been used in an editorial manner without any intent to convey endorsement of or other affiliation with the name claimant. Neither the author nor the publisher intends to express any judgment as to the validity or legal status of any such proprietary claims.

McGraw-Hill books are available at special quantity discounts to use as premiums and sales promotions, or for use in corporate training programs. To contact a representative, please e-mail us at bulksales@mcgraw-hill.com.

This book is printed on acid-free paper.

Contents

Preface

I have long written articles for "those who are crisis managers, whether they want to be or not," which became the slogan of my *Crisis Manager* newsletter. If you've purchased this book, you probably fit that description.

Few managers are trained to deal with the wide variety of crises that can threaten lives, reputation, and an organization's bottom line. While lawyers can do their best to protect you in and out of court, the fact is that your business can go down the tubes long before the legal wrangling is over if you don't have at least basic crisis management skills.

That's what you'll find in *Manager's Guide to Crisis Management*—the basic skills and knowledge you need to deal with the crises that inevitably emerge in any business or organization.

The book begins by giving you a primer that you might find useful in convincing your superiors (if you aren't already in the C-suite) of the importance of crisis management. It then moves into the art of crisis *prevention*—always cheaper than crisis *response* (Chapter 2)—followed by chapters educating you about crisis planning (Chapter 3), crisis training (Chapter 4), and crisis drills (Chapter 5) to keep you sharp.

After that, you'll get into the meat of crisis response (Chapter 6) and then segue into chapters on crisis-related messaging (Chapter 7) and recovering from a crisis (Chapter 8). The chapters that follow address some specific crisis management challenges:

- Online reputation management (Chapter 9)
- Interaction of crisis management PR and the law (Chapter 10)
- Crisis management for public companies (Chapter 11)
- Cultural issues in crisis management (Chapter 12)

Want to know what tools can make your crisis prevention and response easier? Good, there's a chapter that answers that question (Chapter 13). Then, at the risk of sounding self-serving, I would be remiss if I didn't offer you some guidelines on when and how to hire a crisis management consultant (Chapter 14). That's followed by a chapter on special crisis management risks (Chapter 15), like when you're specifically targeted by the media, or targeted for an official investigation.

Finally, in Chapter 16, "Moral Imperatives and the Future of Crisis Management," I address some of the core realities of my trade, make some projections for our future, and suggest how *you* fit into all that.

You may be a crisis manager whether you want to be or not, but after reading this book a time or two, you'll be a much better one.

Special Features

The idea behind the books in the Briefcase series is to give you practical information written in a friendly person-to-person style. The chapters deal with tactical issues and include lots of examples. They also feature numerous sidebars designed to give you different types of specific information. Here's an overview of the types of sidebars and what they cover.

KEY TERM Every subject has some jargon, including this one, dealing with crisis management. These sidebars provide definitions of terms and concepts as they are introduced.

SMART MANAGING These sidebars do just what their name suggests: give you tips and tactics for using the ideas in this book to intelligently manage through the use of effective crisis management principles and practices.

Tricks of the Trade sidebars give you insider how-to hints on techniques astute managers use to execute the tactics described in this book.

It's always useful to have examples that show how the principles in the book are applied. These sidebars provide descriptions of on-the-job situations where effective crisis management improves your response and results.

Caution sidebars provide warnings for where things could go wrong when dealing with crises so you can anticipate and make sure things go well.

How can you make sure you won't make a mistake when you're trying to implement the techniques the book describes? You can't, but these sidebars give you practical advice on how to minimize the possibility of things going wrong.

This icon identifies sidebars where you'll find specific procedures, techniques, or technology you can use to successfully implement the book's principles and practices.

Acknowledgments

I must acknowledge, first and foremost, the man who virtually co-authored this book with me, Bruce Bonafede of Bonafede Communications. He took the time and effort to help me organize what I've learned and occasionally innovated during my almost three decades in crisis management public relations. Without his writing skills and dedicated effort, you would not be reading this publication.

I also want to express my appreciation to John Woods of CWL Publishing, who developed McGraw-Hill's Briefcase Book series and sought me out to author this text.

To all my clients over the years, thank you for letting me be of service to you.

And to my eternal muse, my wife Celeste, much love and gratitude for your patience when I had to put work before pleasure.

Manager's Guide
to Crisis Management

The Importance of Crisis Management

What is *Crisis Management*? It's the art of avoiding trouble when you can, and reacting appropriately when you can't.

That's about as simple as it gets. From that definition you can see that crisis management could apply to business situations, to psychological issues, even to problems at home. But the type of crisis management we're talking about in this book has its closest correlation to firefighting.

Every year, tens of thousands of brave firefighters earn headlines for their efforts at fighting fires, as well they should—they save lives, homes, and businesses whenever they can. But the guys rolling on the fire engines are not, in fact, the ones who save us the most money every year. It's the fire inspectors who do that. The fire prevention work of fire inspectors goes on every day, and it goes on unheralded, but in fact it saves more lives, homes, and businesses than do the heroic actions of their firefighting brethren.

That's why, for organizational purposes, we need to define crisis management as the art of preventing loss when possible and minimizing loss when it's not.

Why is crisis management an art and not a science? Because there are no formulas that can be applied to all cases and guarantee success. The number and variety of crises to which any organization is potentially subject is almost limitless. Environmental disasters, legal challenges, employee misbehaviors,

Crisis Any situation that's threatening or could threaten to harm people or property, seriously interrupt business, damage reputation, and/or negatively impact share value.

KEY TERM

labor disputes, supply chain interruptions, product defects, consumer activism, the leaking of proprietary information—the list goes on and on. There are, of course, proven courses of action that, when followed, will help ward off such crises or mitigate their impact—they are the subject of this book—but there's no "one size fits all" approach that can immunize you or your organization against crises.

Types of Crises

While there are myriad examples of different kinds of crises, they can be divided into three general categories:

- **Creeping Crises:** foreshadowed by a series of events that decision makers don't view as part of a pattern
- **Slow-Burn Crises:** have given some advance warning, but the situation has not yet caused any actual damage
- **Sudden Crises:** the damage has already occurred and will get worse the longer it takes to respond

SMART MANAGING

WATCH THE CREEPERS
It's not uncommon for what seems to be a sudden crisis to have actually, first, been a creeping crisis that wasn't detected. Appropriate measures, early in the process, can often prevent or, at least, minimize the damage from slow-burn and sudden crises.

Here are some examples of crises from the healthcare industry. You should be able to develop comparable lists for your industry.

Creeping Crises
- Lack of a rumor-control system, resulting in damaging rumors
- Inadequate preparation for partial or complete business interruption
- Inadequate steps to protect life and property in the event of emergencies
- Inadequate two-way communication with all audiences, internal and external

Slow-Burn Crises

- Internet activism
- Most lawsuits
- Most discrimination complaints
- Company reputation
- Lack of regulatory compliance—safety, immigration, environment, hiring, permits, etc.
- Major operational decisions that may distress any important audience, internal or external
- Local/state/national governmental actions that negatively impact operations
- Official/governmental investigations involving your healthcare organization and/or any of its employees
- Labor unrest
- Sudden management changes—voluntary or involuntary
- Marketing misrepresentation

Sudden Crises

- Patient death—your healthcare organization perceived to be liable in some way
- Patient condition worsened—your healthcare organization perceived to be liable in some way
- Serious on-site accident
- Insane/dangerous behavior by anyone at a location controlled by your healthcare organization
- Criminal activity at a company site and/or committed by company employees
- Lawsuits with no advance notice or clue whatsoever
- Natural disasters
- Loss of workplace/business interruption (for any reason)
- Fires
- Perceptions of significant impropriety that damage reputation and/or result in legal liability, e.g., publicized involvement of company employee in a group or activity perceived to be a threat to the U.S. government or society; inappropriate comments by a "loose cannon"; business activities not officially authorized by management

Typically, reviewing a list like this triggers thoughts of other situations that need to be addressed during the crisis planning process.

What Is a Stakeholder?

A *stakeholder* is anyone or any organization that, logically, has a vested interest, "a stake," in what happens to your organization.

No organization can function, let alone succeed, without the implicit if not the explicit support of its stakeholders. It certainly can't stand against their outright opposition. This is what crisis management is all about: retaining the support of stakeholders during adverse circumstances.

Stakeholders can be both internal and external. Let's look at some examples.

Internal Stakeholders
- Employees
- Family members of employees
- Board of directors
- Union leadership

External Stakeholders
- Investors
- Customers or clients
- Suppliers
- Referral sources
- Influencers in the investment community
- Community leaders
- Regulators
- Legislators
- Media serving all of the above

How Crisis Management Can Benefit Your Business or Organization

Traditional marketing and public relations (PR) exist to promote the value of an organization, but when the stuff hits the fan, you need to be able to stop the value from plummeting. The purpose of crisis manage-

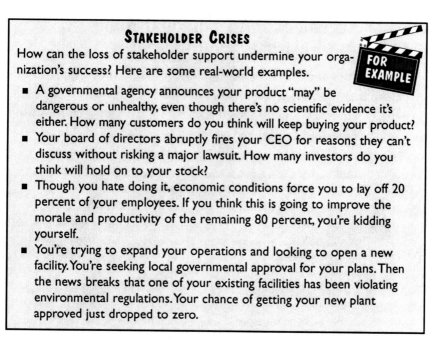

STAKEHOLDER CRISES

How can the loss of stakeholder support undermine your organization's success? Here are some real-world examples.

- A governmental agency announces your product "may" be dangerous or unhealthy, even though there's no scientific evidence it's either. How many customers do you think will keep buying your product?
- Your board of directors abruptly fires your CEO for reasons they can't discuss without risking a major lawsuit. How many investors do you think will hold on to your stock?
- Though you hate doing it, economic conditions force you to lay off 20 percent of your employees. If you think this is going to improve the morale and productivity of the remaining 80 percent, you're kidding yourself.
- You're trying to expand your operations and looking to open a new facility. You're seeking local governmental approval for your plans. Then the news breaks that one of your existing facilities has been violating environmental regulations. Your chance of getting your new plant approved just dropped to zero.

ment is to preserve what has been gained through promotion, marketing, customer service, distribution, and quality control. That's why costs associated with crisis management, either prevention or response, should logically be perceived as an investment, not an expense.

There are numerous ways crisis management can help an organization facing a crisis:

OUNCE OF PREVENTION... SMART

There's been research that shows that for every $1 invested in crisis management—prevention, training, or response—an organization avoids $7 in losses! That type of return should make even the stingiest bean-counter happy.

MANAGING

- Retain goodwill, that intangible asset necessary to the functioning of every organization
- Shore up employee morale
- Minimize the impacts of negative media coverage
- Stave off governmental actions that can cause further challenges
- Protect business operations
- Retain investor confidence

Crisis Management and Traditional Public Relations—Similarities and Differences

Most companies and organizations understand the need for public relations, and they're aware of the benefits such efforts can have. As a result, they direct some funding into such efforts. But without a crisis staring them in the face they're less likely to invest in crisis preparedness.

They don't see that their priorities are entirely backward.

SMART MANAGING

THE RIGHT CHANNELS

Crisis management focuses on traditional and social media far less than PR does. That's because you can't control the message 100 percent via the media, but you can manage it 100 percent through channels you control, e.g., business-to-business (B2B) communications, websites, blogs, direct mail/e-mail.

This isn't to say that in a crisis you should ignore your stakeholders. Just the opposite. Any sound crisis management plan allows for feedback from stakeholders. It's more about getting your own messages out as you want them communicated. When you're dependent on the media to do that you're far less likely to be successful. As you'll see below, the tactics of crisis communications and traditional PR can be very different.

Here are some other ways PR and crisis management are similar and yet differ:

- Both activities use the media, but PR focuses a lot more on traditional and social media than does crisis management.
- PR is proactive. Crisis management, at least in its response mode, is reactive.
- PR seeks media exposure that is 100 percent positive. Crisis management seeks media exposure that is as balanced as possible; meaning you can expect no more than 50 percent of any coverage to be on your side. But in a crisis that's a lot better than 100 percent against you.
- PR is about building an image. Crisis management is about protecting that image.
- PR is done in a threat-less environment. As a result, its successes are typically underappreciated. Crisis management is done in a threatening environment. When the crisis is over management, having

> **Public relations** The actions of a business, organization, government, individual, etc., in promoting goodwill between itself and the public, the community, employees, customers, etc.
>
> **KEY TERMS**
>
> **Crisis management** The art of preventing or minimizing business or organizational loss when threatened by a crisis.
>
> As the definitions show, crisis management can best be seen as a subset of public relations. But it is not strictly PR because its goal is different. It does not seek to promote goodwill as much as seek to preserve goodwill when that asset is threatened by a crisis.

stared into the abyss, it is usually chastened and ready to invest in preventing further crises.

The point is PR and crisis management are not the same. They share some tactics, but rarely strategies, because they don't share the same goals.

Crisis Management and the C-Suite

Let's talk about crisis management and what's commonly called the C-Suite, your top corporate executives. The fact is that every employee has a role in crisis management, whether he or she wants it, because every employee is a representative (at some level) of the organization.

But the leadership of the crisis management process must come from the top leadership of any organization. If it doesn't, it's doomed to fail. Because when a crisis hits an organization must put its A-team forward to maximize its chances of success.

Members of the C-Suite typically become the members of what is commonly called the core crisis communications team. Often, the lead spokespeople for the organization come from the levels of senior or executive vice president or higher. To be fully prepared, that means that each of them, just like you, will have to make time in their already-busy calendars to learn how to be effective crisis managers.

Today, very few of us work for organizations with C-Suites that have fully embraced the need for comprehensive crisis preparedness and all that entails. You may, in fact, play a pivotal role in introducing this idea to your CEO and his or her topic advisors.

I know it's not easy. I've spent almost 30 years attempting to convince

C-Suite types why crisis preparedness is a sound investment. And I've had varying success. Those who have listened have come through crises that otherwise would have sunk their organizations. Those who haven't listened have suffered unnecessary consequences.

There's some element of human nature that argues, unconsciously I think, against crisis preparedness. It's the same thing I notice among many who live where I live—Southern California—and who refuse to prepare themselves for a major earthquake.

I call it the "ostrich effect," and if you look at my eZine, The Crisis Manager, you'll notice it's our main graphic. It's an image of humor, but also of foolishness.

CAUTION

HEAD IN THE SAND

Here are some samples of ostrich behavior. These are actual comments heard in crisis-related senior management meetings:

- "We're not doing anything everybody else hasn't done."
- "People will understand we didn't mean any harm."
- "I know it's better, but we can't afford to do it that way."
- "The media haven't called. Let's not do anything until they do."
- "Let's not address it and upset everyone. That'll only make it worse."
- "No, I don't want you to call them back. I don't care if they're from [CNN, 60 Minutes, The Wall Street Journal ... pick one]."

Don't let the ostriches run your organization. If they were right, would they have to keep their heads in the sand?

The reality is with today's media-saturated society, and a 60/24/7 news cycle (forget TV; with the Internet news is now instantaneous), there's no organization on the planet that isn't vulnerable to a crisis of some kind. Even if it hasn't done anything wrong.

The good news is there are ways to prepare. And ways to respond. You and your organization aren't helpless. There are ways to manage the unmanageable. That's what this book will show you.

Manager's Checklist for Chapter 1

☑ Crisis management is the art of avoiding trouble when you can, and reacting appropriately when you can't.

☑ There are three types of crises: creeping, slow-burn, and sudden.

☑ Stakeholders are the basis of any organization. Crisis management aims to retain their loyalty during adverse circumstances.

☑ A balanced story is the best you can hope for in a crisis.

☑ Crisis management is similar to, but different from, traditional PR.

☑ C-Suite senior management must buy in to crisis management for it to succeed.

☑ Crisis management preserves the value of your organization. It's an investment.

Crisis Prevention

Crisis management is not a single activity. There are, in fact, several levels of activity that fall under the umbrella term "crisis management." They are, in the typical order of activities:

- Crisis prevention
- Crisis planning
- Crisis training
- Crisis response
- Crisis recovery

This is the order of activities because generally one activity leads to the next. We'll look at each of these in turn, and some others, but in this chapter our focus is on crisis prevention.

> **Crisis prevention** The examination of organizational operations under threat-based scenarios in order to find and fix operational and communications weaknesses.
>
> **KEY TERM**

The Best Way to Manage a Crisis Is to Prevent It

To refer to the analogy at the beginning of Chapter 1, crisis management is as much like fire prevention as it is firefighting. Just as the resources needed to prevent a fire pale in comparison to those needed to fight one (not to mention the danger involved), the resources needed to prevent a

SMART MANAGING

INAPPROPRIATE DEFENSE

Never defend your company and/or its employees "at all costs." Humans make mistakes; everyone understands that. Mature businesspeople acknowledge their mistakes, quickly make appropriate apologies and amends, and often save the customer/client relationship.

crisis are far less than those that need to be mustered once a crisis has broken out.

Crisis prevention costs are always a tiny fraction of the losses typically incurred as a result of crises for which there has been inadequate preparation. I've seen many companies and organizations incur millions of dollars in legal, operational, and public relations/marketing costs as the result of a crisis that could have been avoided with adequate preparation.

The Best Way to Prevent a Crisis Is to Anticipate It

Just as the best way to manage a crisis is to prevent it, the best way to

CAUTION

EVEN ONCE IS TOO MUCH

You never know how doing a disservice to a single customer can backfire on you because of the power of the Internet. It's bad enough when people without a legitimate complaint make waves on sites like RipOff Report, but when the complaint comes from a credible source the damage can be considerable and often not fully reversible.

prevent a crisis is to anticipate it and correct its potential causes in advance. You can't anticipate every conceivable crisis your organization might face, but you *can* greatly improve your odds of avoiding many of them—and enhance your ability to survive unavoidable ones.

The most cost-effective way to anticipate the types of

crises your organization is vulnerable to is to conduct a Vulnerability Audit. This is, at its best, the organizational equivalent of a full-blown fire inspection.

Typically a vulnerability audit is best done with an outside consultant, someone who can help you look at your organization and its operations with fresh eyes. Another advantage is that an experienced crisis management consultant will be able to spot many of the "red flags" that can indicate the potential for future crises, or that can exacerbate existing issues.

In an audit, ideally, every functional area of a client organization is examined to identify anything that could lead to a significant interruption in business and/or to reputation damage. The scope of a vulnerability audit can vary depending on client preferences and needs. Some options include:

> **Vulnerability audit** A multidisciplinary risk assessment to determine current and potential areas **KEY TERM** of operational and communications weakness and strength, and to identify potential solutions, because weaknesses may result in emergencies or crises of varying magnitudes if not corrected. An audit is conducted not only to prepare clients for potential crises, but to make them crisis-resistant.

Crisis Document Audit. A simple (typically 5–10 hour) review of existing client documents related to crisis preparedness and response, such as crisis communications plans, emergency response policies, disaster plans, etc. This audit includes creation of a written evaluation and recommendations for improvement.

Executive Session Vulnerability Audit. A one-day session (typically 10–15 hours, inclusive of prep time) in which the client's executive team is led through a series of educational and thought-provoking discussions to uncover and begin to address organizational vulnerabilities that could escalate to crises. This audit includes a post-session written summary of findings and recommendations for improvement.

Comprehensive Vulnerability Audit. A series of interviews with employees at all levels of an organization (typically 60–70 hours total, inclusive of prep time), each conducted in complete confidence so that the interviewee feels comfortable disclosing information he/she might not otherwise discuss. This is complemented by interviews with representative members of key external audiences, and concludes with preparation and presentation of a comprehensive audit report to the senior management team.

Blended Vulnerability Audit. An Executive Session Vulnerability Audit as a starting point, supplemented by a limited number of selective one-on-one interviews (typically totaling 20–30 hours, inclusive of prep time).

Online Reputation Management Audit. A comprehensive review of the client's current online presence, visibility, and vulnerability to reputation attacks online, concluding with specific recommendations for significant improvement (typically 15–20 hours). The audit includes the use of sophisticated analysis and report-generating software. The detail is provided at a level useful to the organization's top executives in marketing/PR, Web design, and information technology.

Typical Audit Questions

The range of questions posed during an audit is too extensive to include here, but some typical questions would be: If your primary place of business was completely unavailable as of midnight tonight—and you had no advance warning:

- Would everyone who works there know where to report for work tomorrow and/or how to conduct business remotely?
- Do you have alternative worksites already identified and contingency plans established that would allow you to move in rapidly?
- Do you have contact information for *all* your key audiences, internal and external, that is available to you quickly even if you were never able to occupy your primary place of business again? Was the information reviewed and updated in the past 90 days?

This is a small sample of the questions I typically ask in a vulnerability audit. If you know your vulnerabilities in advance, you can avoid many crises and most certainly minimize the damage from others.

How a Vulnerability Audit Is Conducted

Data are collected from people in key information flow positions. Senior executives are not always aware of all of the circumstances that can lead to the birth of a crisis. Hence, interviews are conducted with both white- and blue-collar personnel at various echelons of the company, typically a minimum of 20 interviews. Multilocation businesses usually require interviews with remote location personnel who have insights specific to their area.

These interviews are conducted on a confidential basis. Ideally, interviewees are told that the firm's senior management will not, under any circumstances, be told "who said what." Information gleaned during the interview process includes (1) potentially harmful trends (facts or perceptions reported by multiple sources); (2) significant inconsistencies between answers from different subjects; (3) nonverbal cues that there may be something amiss in certain areas, which then prompts further questioning; and (4) consensus opinion regarding the probability of certain types of crises.

The focus is on operational and communications weaknesses that could cause or contribute to a crisis. An employee who's a "loose cannon" is a more obvious potential source of problems, even if he/she is well intentioned, but there are less obvious issues revealed through the vulnerability audit process. For example, one past client relied on a single fax machine for incoming and outgoing faxes from its headquarters offices during a crisis, which tremendously delayed communication with a number of important audiences. The simple addition of fax machines, creation of broadcast fax/e-mail lists, and similar tactics can often greatly improve crisis response.

The audit allows you to anticipate actual crisis scenarios. Every organization is vulnerable to certain types of crises inherent in the nature of its business, plus others inherent, perhaps, in the nature of its particular style of operating. Additionally, the vulnerability audit has been known to reveal "skeletons" of which senior management may have been unaware.

The conclusions from the vulnerability audit are then analyzed and presented both as an in-person briefing and in writing as follows:

Recommendations for systems revisions. If there are changes (such as the addition of backup communications systems) that can optimize crisis prevention and response, they are recommended.

Discussion of scenarios most likely to affect the client company. The audit will lead to a list of "most likely" scenarios with which the organization may deal in the future. At the in-person presentation of audit results, that list is finalized (which often results in deletion or addition of some scenarios) and then the management team brainstorms both general and audience-specific key messages for each scenario.

The information collected in the vulnerability audit process is used as the basis for writing a manual that will guide the entire organization in the communications aspects of responding to crisis situations, to include clear delineation of individual responsibilities and draft responses that reflect the company's values while considering the public's sensitivities and need to know.

Once an organization has undergone a vulnerability audit, it's likely to see several important (and money-saving) benefits. Operational and other weaknesses can be corrected and crises prevented before they happen. Response time for a crisis is dramatically enhanced. And if a crisis does occur, the cost to the organization is typically greatly reduced.

One would think that, given those benefits, an audit would be an automatic part of the business planning process. Perhaps one day it will be but, for now, fewer than 5 percent of organizations I've encountered have undergone the crisis vulnerability audit and crisis plan creation process. More common is the purchase and adaptation of an "off the shelf" crisis plan. How good are they? Well, would you run your business on an off-the-shelf business plan?

Do-It-Yourself Audits

If your organization is small, or you're just beginning to get your feet wet as a crisis manager, there are two other approaches you can take that can add great value to your crisis preparedness.

First, you can conduct an informal "Walkabout Vulnerability Audit" of your organization by following these steps:

1. Examine the contents of at least 10 unsecured trash cans after a busy day at work. See if you find information you would not want to find in the hands of competitors, which would compromise you legally and/or which would be embarrassing if revealed to a customer or the general public.

2. Ask 10 employees, at random, how comfortable they would be with you reading "anything" they might have on their company-owned computers. If they're not, hand them another copy of your most-excellent computer security policy. You do have one, of course?

3. Sit down at any organizational computer left on after-hours. See if the user is still logged in (exposing every file to which he/she has access).

4. Listen to conversations coming out of offices, cubicles, or in the halls. What would you think of them if you were a visiting reporter, customer, or client?

5. Make a round of the four most popular lunchtime restaurants and/or after-work drink hangouts frequented by your employees. Listen for "loose lips" and "loose cannons" who may be inadvertently giving away sensitive information where anyone might hear it. Not to finger them, but so that you can determine if it's a trend that needs to be addressed with better policies and training.

6. See how strong your visitor security policies really are. If you require visitors to sign in and sign out, take a look at your sign-in log sometime and see how many actually do both. If you require Visitor guest badges, do you see Visitors going down the hall alone and never being challenged? And are all your badges accounted for?

7. Ask the right person at your shop "Hey, how often do we change out the main entrance locks?" and/or "How often do we change passwords for each employee?" The answer to both, if you don't want to invite crises, should be at least twice a year.

A Case History: Audit Benefits

I am aware of a healthcare company that operated for over 10 years without a significant crisis, and then experienced a number of crises over a short period of time. Some of these situations, lacking proper response, could have resulted in significant damage to the firm's credibility and profitability.

Fortunately, and very atypically, the organization had recently commissioned a crisis communications plan that provided them with a system for coordinated, prompt, honest, informative, and concerned response to crises. This plan consisted not only of a manual with scenarios and instructions, but also involved a comprehensive audit of the organization's vulnerabilities that resulted in numerous recommendations for operational/system changes, which, if unchanged, created a potential for crises.

For example, the audit and subsequent analysis (conducted over a six-week period) revealed a lack of standard procedures on how to route media calls and who should handle the calls. Yet, particularly during a crisis, all employees need to know to whom a reporter should be referred or else a number of "loose cannons" are likely to be quoted instead of trained, authorized spokespersons.

Additionally, there were no fixed policies on some controversial issues such as the interaction of HIV-positive employees with patients nor was there a standard procedure for responding to needle sticks by medical personnel. This lack of policy could have resulted in significant criticism or worse, and the recommendations made during the crisis planning process ensured that the crisis would not happen. In some cases, the board of directors or administrative staff were aware of system weaknesses but hadn't thought of the communications/bottom-line impact of failure to quickly correct the problems.

Prevention, versus reaction, is the ultimate key to successful crisis management. How many of my clients conduct an audit or create a crisis plan *before* having a significant crisis? Less than 5 percent. That's because they look at the one-time cost (typically $20,000 or more for a single small- to mid-sized firm) and choose to avoid impacting their budget today versus giving significant thought to the fiscal impact of a crisis that could happen tomorrow. I am usually asked to do an audit *after* a damaging crisis, during which we spend considerable time, at client expense, attempting to minimize damage, "fire fighting" in a crisis management sense that very likely would have been unnecessary if an audit had been done and a crisis plan were in place. Yes, crisis communications counsel will be needed even if a plan has been created, but far less of it. In conclusion: Crises will occur, and they can be *very* damaging to your organization. But there is a tactic available that can eliminate many crises and minimize the impact of others.

Just as there are fire marshals.

Manager's Checklist for Chapter 2

☑ The best way to manage a crisis is to prevent it.

☑ The best way to prevent a crisis is through a vulnerability audit.

☑ There are several kinds of audits.

☑ You can do an audit yourself.

Crisis Planning

O nce you have a comprehensive list of your organization's vulnerabilities—either by developing it yourself or by bringing in an
outside consultant to assist you—your next step is writing your
crisis plan.

And yes, I said *writing* your plan. The idea that you can get by in a crisis because "we all know what to do" is guaranteed to lead to organizational chaos. "Winging it" is not a crisis plan. Responsibilities, protocols,
actions, messages, and more must all be spelled out clearly so there is no
confusion in the heat of the moment.

Get it all down in writing, circulate it to ensure consensus, tweak as
necessary, then *use* it (I talk more about that in the next chapters).

Is there a format you should follow? No. Is there a template you can
use? Yes and no. There are crisis plan templates available (for free) on the
Internet, but I've yet to find one I think has value for real-world applica-
tion. More importantly, I'm generally not in favor of "template" crisis
plans; I believe their "fill in the blanks" approach is antithetical to the
kind of rigorous thinking writing a crisis plan *should* entail.

Then what should a crisis plan include? Here are the primary components.

Crisis Plan Essentials

Here is a review of what you'll find in a sound crisis plan.

Table of Contents/Index. Include both a Table of Contents at the beginning of the plan and an Index at the end. In a crisis these will make it easier for team members to access the section most relevant or most needed by them.

Introductory Statements. An introduction, plus statements of the purpose, scope, relevant policies, and goals of the plan will help keep you on track in determining what to include and what to leave out.

Documentation. Provide a section for the crisis team to keep detailed logs of actions taken during a crisis. Facts related to the situation, meeting minutes, decisions made, actions taken, and justification for any deviations from policy should be recorded. Detailed records of media contacts and all information released to the media should also be maintained.

Emergency Operations Center. An Emergency Operations Center (or in some cases more than one) for use by the crisis management team should be selected and included in the plan. Include the location, location details, and available communications infrastructure.

The Core Crisis Management Team. A small team of senior executives should be identified to serve as your company's core crisis management team. Ideally, the team will be led by the company or organization's CEO, with the firm's top public relations executive and legal counsel as his or her chief advisers. If your in-house PR executive does not have sufficient crisis communications expertise, he or she may choose to retain an agency or independent consultant with that specialty. Other team members should be the heads of major organizational divisions, to include finance, personnel, and operations. Include all contact information for all media (phone, fax, cell, e-mail, social media).

Team Member Responsibilities. Include all team members' roles and responsibilities in the event of a crisis.

Supplemental Teams. If your company or organization has multiple locations, you may consider having each location or branch maintain its own crisis team that reports to the headquarters team. Again, include all contact information.

Alternate Team Members. Many crisis plans break down in this area. They assign a person to their relevant crisis role, but when the crisis hits the person is unavailable or out of contact. Your plan should include an alternate for each member of your crisis team(s) with their contact information.

Team Resource Requirements. A listing of the communications infrastructure needed to maintain contact between team members during a crisis—no matter where they are.

Crisis Procedures and Holding Statements for Each Scenario. One tabbed section for each crisis scenario in the plan (based, hopefully, on your vulnerability audit). Procedures will include instructions for internal and external communications. While full message development must await the outbreak of an actual crisis, "holding statements" (messages designed for use immediately after a crisis breaks) can be developed in advance to be used for a wide variety of scenarios to which the organization is perceived to be vulnerable. An example of holding statements by a hotel chain with properties hit by a natural disaster—before the company headquarters has any hard factual information—might be:

- "We have implemented our crisis response plan, which places the highest priority on the health and safety of our guests and staff."
- "Our hearts and minds are with those who are in harm's way, and we hope that they are well."
- "We will be supplying additional information when it is available and posting it on our website."

The organization's crisis team should regularly review holding statements to determine if they require revision and/or whether statements for other scenarios should be developed.

Spokespersons. Within each team, there should be individuals who are the only ones authorized to speak for the company or organization in times of crisis. The CEO should be one of those spokespersons, but not necessarily the primary spokesperson. The fact is that some chief executives are brilliant businesspeople but not very effective in-person communicators. The decision about who should speak is made after a crisis breaks, but the pool of potential spokespersons should be identified and trained in advance.

Not only are spokespersons needed for media communications, but for all types and forms of communications, internal and external, including on-camera, at a public meeting, at employee meetings, etc. You really don't want to be making decisions about so many different types of spokespersons while "under fire."

Spokesperson Training. Two typical quotes from well-intentioned company executives summarize the reason why your spokespersons should receive professional training in how to speak to the media:

- "I talked to that nice reporter for over an hour and he didn't use the most important news about my organization."
- "I've done a lot of public speaking. I won't have any trouble at that public hearing."

Regarding the first example, there are a good number of Lesley Stahl *60 Minutes* victims who thought they knew how to talk to the press. In the second case, most executives who have attended a hostile public hearing have gone home wishing they had been wearing a pair of Depends.

All stakeholders—internal and external—are just as capable of misunderstanding or misinterpreting information about your organization as the media is, and it's your responsibility to minimize the chance of that happening.

We'll talk more about media training in another chapter, but the point here is *put it in the plan.*

Communications Protocols. Initial crisis-related news can be received at any level of a company. A janitor may be the first to know there is a problem, or someone in personnel, or notification could be in the form of a midnight phone call from an out-of-town executive. Who should be notified, and where do you reach them?

An emergency communications "tree" should be established and distributed to all company employees, telling them precisely what to do and whom to call if there appears to be a potential for or an actual crisis. In addition to appropriate supervisors, at least one member of the crisis communications team, plus an alternate member, should include their cell-phone, office, and home phone numbers on the emergency contact list.

Some companies prefer not to use the term "crisis," thinking that this may cause panic. Frankly, using "potentially embarrassing situations" or similar phrases doesn't fool anyone. Particularly if you prepare in advance, your employees will learn that "crisis" doesn't even necessarily mean "bad news," but simply "very important to our company, act quickly."

Stakeholder Section. Who are the stakeholders that matter to your organization? Most organizations, for example, care about their employees, customers, prospects, suppliers, and the media. Private

> ## COMMUNICATIONS TREE
> **TRICKS OF THE TRADE**
>
> A communications "tree" is called that because when sketched out it resembles ... well, a tree. Think of a pine tree, narrow at the top and broadening toward the bottom. Trees can be used for a number of purposes including reporting the outbreak of a crisis or a potential crisis, but also for the crisis team to communicate messages to the rest of management. Smart crisis managers try to design that sort of tree so that no one person has to communicate with more than two others, then they each communicate with two more, etc. This way neither you nor your CEO has to call every manager in the organization. Let the tree do it.

investors may be involved. Publicly held companies have to comply with Securities and Exchange Commission and stock exchange information requirements, and will probably want to include institutional shareholders, analysts, investment firms, and influential bloggers on finance. Or, your organization may answer to local, state, or federal regulatory agencies.

You *must* include the members of all these audiences in your crisis plan, segregated by their type of stakeholder.

Communications Methods. For each stakeholder group, you need to have, in advance, complete e-mailing, snail-mailing, fax, and phone number lists to accommodate rapid communication in time of crisis. And you need to know what type of information each stakeholder group is seeking, as well as the best way to reach each of your contacts.

Another thing to consider is whether you have an automated system established to ensure rapid communication with those stakeholders. You should also think about backup communications options such as toll-free numbers for emergency call-ins or special websites that can be activated in times of crisis to keep various stakeholders informed and/or to conduct online incident management.

Consider these factors in advance, build them into your plan, and rapid communication during crises will be relatively easy.

Summary Section. In your plan, include a Summary section where you will record the results of the "post-mortem" you will hold following your crisis to critique the plan and its strengths and weaknesses.

EFFECTIVE NOTIFICATION

TOOLS A notification system is a combination of software and hardware that provides a means of delivering a message to a set of recipients. For example, a notification system can send an e-mail when a new topic has been added to a website, i.e., your latest public statement on a crisis.

There are some services that make it possible, for a price, to send broadcast notifications out to stakeholders using multiple contact systems, e.g., phone, e-mail, text, and receive confirmation that the message was received.

But just like the "phone trees" my clients were using 25 years ago, a notification system is only as good as the contact information available. And they are not foolproof; the information can be wrong, entered incorrectly, or simply out of date.

On top of all that, notification systems are subject to violating laws or blacklisting by third parties that transmit the information if they are viewed as spam. If using a notification system, an opt-in process of collecting data protects the system from unlawful use, because each recipient is giving the system permission to contact him or her. However, it still may not reach everyone on your contact list.

Anticipate Crises

If you *haven't* conducted any kind of vulnerability audit—by now you'll wish you had—gather your crisis team for long brainstorming sessions on all the potential crises that can occur at your organization. There are at least two immediate benefits to this exercise:

You may realize that some of the situations are preventable by simply modifying existing methods of operation.

You can begin to think about possible responses, about best case/worst case scenarios, etc. Better now than when under the pressure of an actual crisis.

BEFORE IT BECOMES PUBLIC

Don't make the mistake of only starting work on a potential crisis after it's become public. Even if you've decided you won't play ostrich, you can still foster your developing crisis by deciding not to do any advance preparation. Before the situation becomes public, you still have some proactive options available. You could, for example, thrash out and even test some planned key messages so that you'll communicate promptly and credibly when the crisis breaks publicly. This will help avoid addressing the issue from a defensive posture.

Use the scenarios you've developed as the basis for all forms of training and drills, as discussed further in Chapter 5.

LOOK AT CONSEQUENCES

A crisis plan needs to be consequence-focused versus scenario-focused. For example, there are many scenarios that could result in catastrophic loss of one's primary facility, but the basic consequence is the same for all. In other words, don't write three separate plans for losing your corporate headquarters to a fire, and a flood, and an earthquake—though you should include each as a scenario within your *single* plan. Again, be cognizant of the threat scenarios you face, but focus on the *result* of these scenarios, not their cause.

Don't Go Plan Crazy

When assessed during the vulnerability process, one prominent West Coast university was found to have no less than six crisis-related plans, each of them created by different employees without any coordination among the originating departments. The documents included:

- Natural disaster response plan
- Facilities emergency plan
- Fire response plan
- Crisis communications plan
- Emergency operations plan
- Web emergency plan

As a result of this haphazard approach to planning, there were gaping holes in crisis preparedness as well as some significant self-inflicted wounds. For example, during a natural disaster such as an earthquake, different plans would have had the same senior-level staff member in two different parts of the campus at the same time.

In fact, only two types of crisis plans need to be done:

- Operational: what do we do, who does it, when is it done, etc.
- Communications: what do we say, who says it, how do we get the messages out, etc.

Those are the two types of crisis plans you may need; everything else should be fit into those two modalities.

Evaluating Your Existing Crisis Plan—10 Questions

If you have an existing crisis plan, or if you've just drafted one yourself, here are some questions to ask that will help you make your plan as bullet-proof as possible.

1. Does your plan identify crisis communications team members by position, not merely by name, and clearly delineate their responsibilities? If not, this needs to be spelled out or, in the throes of a crisis, there can be significant and potentially damaging miscommunication.
2. Is your plan current, regularly updated based on changes in the organization as well as by periodic brainstorming sessions about vulnerabilities? If not current, update immediately; contact lists should be updated at least twice annually, the rest of the plan at least annually.
3. Was your plan prepared by someone who is as qualified in his or her field as your specialty field attorneys are in theirs? If not, have the plan reviewed immediately by a qualified individual. A crisis communications plan "off the shelf" or created by an underqualified person is like having a critical legal document prepared by a paralegal without supervision.
4. Was your plan prepared based on a comprehensive vulnerability audit? If not, chances are you missed some vital vulnerabilities that could undermine your planning. Consider having the document upgraded following a vulnerability audit.
5. Does your plan contain draft messages ready to help you respond to

the types of crisis you are most likely to face? If not, create such messages ASAP. The delay in drafting messages from scratch when a crisis is already breaking, not to mention the difficulty due to the "fog of war," can result in damage you could have avoided.

FIND SUPPLIERS AHEAD SMART

If you're likely to need certain types of products or services as a result of the types of crises most common to an MANAGING organization such as yours (e.g., backup generators, testing laboratories), the time to establish relationships with product/service providers is *now*, not under the gun of a crisis. Corollary lesson: During times of widespread crises, such as a natural disaster, demand for certain types of products/services is higher than the supply; "preferred customers" move to the front of the line, last-minute customers may not be served at all.

6. Does your plan consider the "ripple effect" of crises that may start outside your organization, but still affect you? Many otherwise strong plans omit this consideration. For example, if your supplier in China is quarantined due to H1N1, then you may not get the product you need and *your* clients or customers won't get their products either.

7. Do you conduct training and simulations for the people who will be implementing the plan? Training—media training and training on implementing the plan, plus simulations such as desktop exercises—is vital the same way military boot camp prepares soldiers to do their job even when under fire.

8. Do all personnel critical to implementing the plan have a backup for when they're not available? If not, implement a backup system, even if you're thinly staffed. Cross-training is the alternative to having a second person be a backup.

9. Does your plan take into consideration the need to communicate with both internal and external stakeholders? Ensure that you're prepared to communicate both internally and externally. Internal audiences are often your most important, as every employee is a PR rep and crisis manager for your organization *whether you want them to be or not.*

10. Is there a rapid-approval process in place so that documents and other tactics aren't delayed awaiting approval when a crisis breaks? Ensure that a process is in place that's understood by all crisis communications team members.

CAUTION

AVOID GOING STALE

One last point for any crisis management plan: Realize that your plan is never truly "completed." Many organizations forget this, and they rue the error. There are many factors that can make your plan "go stale."

- Changes in personnel
- Changes in vendors, suppliers, and other business partners
- Changes in organizational strategies
- Changes in media contacts
- Changes in laws and regulations affecting your operation

And many others. This is why I say contact lists should be updated at least twice annually; the rest of the plan at least annually. Don't get caught in a crisis you could have avoided if only you'd updated your plan; or not communicating with key stakeholders because nobody thought to add them to your contact lists.

"It Can't Happen To Me"

When a healthy organization's CEO or CFO looks at the cost of preparing a crisis plan, with either a heavy investment of in-house time or retention of an outside consultant for a substantial fee, it's tempting for them to fantasize "it can't happen to me" or "if it happens to me, we can handle it relatively easily."

Hopefully, that type of ostrich-behavior is rapidly becoming a thing of the past. You, or even the best crisis management professional you bring in to help, will be playing serious catch-up—with more damage occurring all the time—if your organization has no crisis communications plan or infrastructure already in place.

Yes, developing a crisis plan takes time and resources. But it's time well spent, and in the long run can save an organization many times more than the initial cost.

Manager's Checklist for Chapter 3

☑ You must *write* your plan to ensure it's effective. Don't think discussing these things is enough.

☑ Don't do a "fill in the blanks" crisis plan. Create your own. Think!

☑ If you already have a crisis plan, vet it based on our 10 questions.

☑ Ideally your organization will have one crisis operations plan and one crisis communications plan—hopefully in a single document covering all scenarios. But if you have more than that, start integrating. Now.

☑ A crisis plan is a living document. Be prepared to update regularly.

Chapter
4

Crisis Training

ongratulations on writing your first crisis plan (or improving the one your organization already had in place). The good news is you've taken an important step in crisis management. The bad news is you're not finished.

A plan is only as good as your ability to put it into action. And that requires training.

A crisis plan that gets written, reviewed, and everyone nods their head and says it's good—and then it gets put on a shelf and nobody looks at it again—is an exercise in futility.

I guarantee that any plan you write that doesn't lead to implementation training will fall to pieces during a crisis. Some team members will follow it, and some won't, which will lead to confusion, conflict, and generally lousy crisis response. Plus a negative reaction from a lot of your stakeholders. So commit to educating your team about the plan you've written, and training them on how to implement it.

What Good Is a Plan Nobody Knows About?

In a crisis, *every* employee is a crisis manager for an organization, whether you want them to be or not. Does every employee know what his or her job is when certain types of crises occur? The job may simply be to refer inquiries to a member of the crisis communications team, but

SMART

MANAGING

REASONS TO TRAIN

There are many reasons to conduct crisis training; among these is the impact on your staff:

- Training helps ensure staff will do what they should, when they should.
- Training prepares your staff to carry out duties they might normally not be expected to and may be unfamiliar with.
- Training helps convince staff that this stuff is important. Let's face it; most of your organization's staff probably aren't involved in crisis preparedness or planning. They may or may not take it all that seriously. But if you require them to undergo training, which gives you the opportunity to explain how it affects them, it might help them understand the importance of these efforts and inspire them to get engaged and help.

the job might also mean getting physically involved with inspecting damaged buildings or calling employees who were home when the tornado hit.

It's not uncommon, unfortunately, for the senior-level members of the crisis communications team or emergency response team (the operational side of things) to be the only ones who know what everyone is expected to do—and then they have to try to find them and ask them to help, while in the midst of a crisis.

The best possible solution, in my opinion, is orientation and refresher training for all employees, coordinated through Human Resources and mandated by organizational leadership.

Members of the response teams, including spokespersons, require more sophisticated levels of training and practice, but no employee should be left out of this process.

Types of Training

There are three types of training that should, ideally, be part of the crisis planning process:

1. Training to the plan.
2. All-staff training.
3. Media/presentation training.

   Let's look at all three.

Training to the Plan

This means sitting down with operational and/or communications team members in person, or virtually through online channels, or some combination of both, for the purpose of going over the crisis plan, page by page, and "talking through" how well they'd work in practice. This is the first "all hands" look at the plan, and invariably elicits both questions and suggestions for improvements. From both a communications and operational perspective this can be an invaluable exercise, since a plan that was written on the basis of certain assumptions can be tightened to meet the needs of the real world, and how operations actually happen and interrelate.

The point is, this doesn't only provide training for staff, it also provides "quality control" for the crisis plan you've written.

All-Staff Training

In keeping with the precept that every employee is a crisis manager for your organization, it's necessary to provide some level of training to all of them. Such training usually covers some basic principles of crisis management, stresses how important each employee is to the process, explains important policies that relate to crisis response (e.g., a designated spokesperson policy), and informs each employee what their role is during certain types of crises based on the plan.

This is also the opportunity to point out to staff that their own self-interest lies in taking the plan seriously. They need to understand the bottom-line impact on them of poor crisis response—i.e., jobs, bonuses, and benefits can all be impacted—so it's in their interest to support the crisis management process.

When conducting this type of training, draw out questions from your staff. Let them know they're welcome to question the plan and its effectiveness. This will not only help engage them, it may also lead to new insights. The reality of any organization is that management doesn't have a monopoly on organizational knowledge. Tap into the awareness of your line or field personnel. It can help you improve your plan.

Media/Presentation Training

Training to communicate with the media or other audiences (e.g., town hall meetings, investor meetings) during times of crisis is significantly different, and harder, than the type of training many spokespersons typically receive to give "soft interviews" to consumer, business, or trade press.

Such crisis media training helps you develop and refine key messages, to see "what really works" under the stress of simulated interviews (and good media trainers make you forget it's simulated); optimizes your chances of achieving balanced coverage; and allows you to identify who should—and who shouldn't—be spokespersons for your organization.

Media Training

For the benefit of readers of this book, I have to say more about media training. It's one of the most important forms of crisis preparedness you can do. Not necessarily that handling the media is more important or valuable than other communications (I talk in Chapter 6 about communicating with audiences without going through the media) but because in a crisis media attention can seem to be your most pressing concern, and, yes, it can have an impact on your other communications. You don't want what you're saying directly to stakeholders to be undermined by something reported in the press.

When I wrote my media training manual several years ago, I titled it *Keeping the Wolves at Bay* for a reason. I used that metaphor to suggest the attitudes and actions of the media in a crisis situation. Do I think all people working in the media today are rapacious, hungry animals? Hardly. Most media people go about their day trying to do their jobs and trying to uphold the ethics of their profession. I have many friends in the media, and so do most of my crisis management colleagues, whom I hold in high regard.

But there's something about a crisis that brings out the worst in many media people. In the interest of getting a scoop, or "scoring the story," or, more likely, improving their professional standing, they throw off the accepted constraints of their profession and "go for the jugular," if you will.

Add to this the need for an organization in a crisis situation to convey its messages of concern and action in a controlled manner, and you can see where the conflicts can arise.

BUDGETS ARE NOT A CONSTRAINT

If your budget simply doesn't allow for outside assistance, and you're conducting all crisis planning and training in-house, insist on realistic media training for your potential spokespeople. Don't just sit and ask them questions; set up a camcorder and watch how they handle themselves on camera. Do they fidget? Do they make eye contact? Do they come across as positive and reassuring, or negative and defensive? This can help you decide whom to actually use to speak to the media and who not. Or, at least who has promise and can be further trained, and who should not be let anywhere near the media.

TRICKS OF THE TRADE

What You Learn from Media Training

There are many things to learn from media training. The main lessons are:

- Your main goal isn't to answer questions; it's to communicate your key messages. Look for ways to get back to those, whatever you're asked.

- Be as positive as possible. Yes, there has been or there is a crisis, but you're here to help deal with it. You're offering a resolution to the problem, comfort to the affected, and information to all those interested. You are doing something positive, so don't act like you don't want to be there.

- You're not speaking for yourself; you're speaking for the organization. So leave your personal feelings and comments for another time.

- It's all right to not have an answer. It's all right to say, "I don't know." But follow it up with "But let me find out and I'll get back to you about that." Then do so.

- If you screw up and say something you didn't mean to, don't panic. Just stop and say, "Wait. That didn't come out the way I meant. What I *meant* to say was . . ."

The key to doing an interview in a crisis situation is to remember you're not there to serve the needs of the media; the media are there to serve yours, or at least those of their viewers, listeners, and readers, who want to hear from you. The reporters' questions are *their* means to that end; they are not yours. So answer them as they suit the needs of your stakeholders, otherwise turn them into something that does.

What Makes a Good Spokesperson?

In a crisis, there is really only one reason to do media interviews, and it's not to answer the media's questions. It's to speak to your stakeholders *through* the media, to use the media as a communications channel to reach your various audiences. (More on this in Chapter 6, when we talk about crisis response.)

But for the purposes of media training, it's important to evaluate, when determining who should be your spokespersons, the following:

- Do they come across as credible? In determining this, don't just listen to their words. Watch their body language, speech patterns, etc.
- Can they keep the key messages front and center?
- Do they seem positive or negative in the spotlight of an interview?
- Are they thrown by challenging questions? (And even if they are, can they be trained not to be?)

Don't Go It Alone

In the current environment of sensational journalism, you can train your organization's spokespeople to deal with the media *if* you have a journalistic background and understand the tricks of the trade. If not, you're really better off bringing in a media training expert who can help you prepare for the media in a crisis.

Yet retaining someone to provide a service about which you know little yourself can always be tricky, whether it be an auto mechanic, lawyer, plumber, computer tech or—the topic du jour—a media trainer.

Here is a list of questions to ask any potential media trainer. I've also included "good answers" that should provide you with insights critical to making an informed decision about using his or her services.

1. Have you been a working journalist yourself?
   Good answer: Yes!
   It's much harder to understand the workings of the media if you haven't spent any time on the "inside," at least at the collegiate and/or intern level.

2. If yes to #1, what type of journalist were you (e.g., anchor, investigative reporter)?

Good answer: Investigative or feature journalists are much more used to "digging" for a story and hence ask more of the tough questions for which you need to prepare. Anchors simply read the news.

3. If no to #1, what is the basis for your understanding of the media?
   Good answer: I made a point of spending part of my PR career actively networking with working journalists.

4. Does your training include how to deal with nontraditional media, e.g., social media?
   Good answer: Yes!

   If the answer is no, say goodbye. Traditional media is no more than 50 percent of the media that will impact you and/or your organization.

5. Will you teach us how we can maintain the skills we have learned from you? Be specific.
   Good answer: Yes. I do that by coming back to conduct refresher training twice a year, teaching you how you can practice on your own.

   One or even two days of media training alone are insufficient to maintain the new skills you're learning—practice is essential.

6. Does your training prepare us for routine interviews and crisis-level interviews?
   Good answer: Yes. We focus X percent of the time on routine interviews and X percent on crisis-level interviews.
   Then you decide if that balance represents your needs.

7. How long have you been a media trainer?
   Good answer: 10 years (or more).

   That said, everyone has to start somewhere. You may find a very skilled trainer with less experience and correspondingly lower pricing, but check their references carefully.

8. Could you show me anything you've written about this topic, and/or articles in which you've been interviewed?
   Good answer: Yes, and I'll get you copies or links right away.

   If someone's good at what they do, they should both publish in that field and make themselves available as media interview subjects.

9. If the stuff hits the fan, can you provide us with spot advice on what we can say?

   Good answer: Yes, I can help craft messaging as well.

   You want to find a person who is more than a trainer, someone you can call on when "the real thing" happens.

10. Are you an experienced media interview subject yourself—i.e., do you practice what you preach?

    Good answer: Yes.

    If you can find media coverage and even video clips featuring your trainer being interviewed, you can see if he/she "walks the talk."

Media Training the Untrainable

Media training is invaluable for anyone who must "dance the dance" with journalists, particularly with regard to crises or sensitive issues. But what do you do when your primary spokesperson, despite many hours of training and practice under the direction of someone skilled in that specialty, still comes out looking like ... (name withheld to avoid embarrassment)?

There are a few variations to this problem:

- The primary spokesperson isn't taking well to training, but there are other potential spokespersons.
- There's truly only one person who should speak about the crisis, he or she does very poorly in training, but he or she is willing to "play to his or her weakness."
- There's truly only one person who should speak about the crisis, but he or she insists that he or she can "handle it."

I have often trained or participated in the training of corporate executives who are part of a two- to four-spokesperson team. Not all crises, and not all media, merit involvement of the CEO or president, but he or she is usually one of those trained. Other senior execs who, by logic of their position or knowledge, are also usually trained, include legal counsel (believe it or not, sometimes we do want the lawyers to comment, specifically on matters of law). In fact, part of what the training helps determine is "who speaks to what subjects."

> ### ALTERNATE SPOKESPERSON
> **SMART**
>
> **MANAGING**
>
> Sometimes, the lead spokesperson cannot be trained to an acceptable level of performance in the time available. There are many possible reasons, the most common of which, in my experience, are fear of the media, hatred of the media, and/or passion about the topic that overrides good judgment. In those cases, I'm candid with my client and suggest that an alternate spokesperson take the lead. I know of more than one CEO who, after media training, pulled himself off the spokesperson team because he knew he'd do more harm than good.

Sometimes things don't work out, but you still might get lucky. If you have only one spokesperson, and he or she is untrainable, but insists, "I can handle it"—pray, and hope there's a competing crisis and no one's paying attention.

Manager's Checklist for Chapter 4

☑ Training means putting your crisis plan into action.

☑ A plan is only worthwhile if people know how to use it.

☑ Types of training involve separate efforts with the crisis team, the staff, and those who will communicate with stakeholders.

☑ You must be trained to deal with today's media.

☑ If you need outside help, vet such help carefully.

Chapter 5

Crisis Drills

Training isn't enough. What do you think would happen to America's military if in the course of their training our soldiers, sailors, airmen, and marines were only *told* what to expect in a combat environment, rather than getting some sense of experiencing it themselves? Similarly, do you think any team in the NFL would have a chance at the SuperBowl if their practices consisted of sitting in meetings and being *told* what to expect when they went out to play the other team? I think their chances would be just about zero.

Training without practice is worthless. Or pretty darn close.

There's a reason for this: It's how we learn. I remember sitting in a parent-teacher's conference and being told by one of my children's teachers, "Kids learn by doing things much better and more easily than they do by just hearing about things."

I had to smile. I wish all my clients understood what this teacher understood. Having a crisis plan for which participants aren't drilled is akin to having a fire evacuation plan with no fire drills; but actually worse, because a crisis management plan is a little more complex than just "Head for the exits."

Potential participants in crisis response need to be formally trained in the basic tenets of crisis management, and then drills or simulations should be conducted to test and refine their newly acquired skills. And repeated periodically to keep them sharp.

How Drills Help

Whether your plan was produced in-house or by an outside agency, conducting realistic simulations of crises that could affect the organization accomplishes many things:

- Drills help ensure employees are capable of effectively implementing them and have the necessary skill sets to respond effectively to unanticipated emergencies.
- Drills help determine if plan elements and strategies that may have been appropriate at the time of plan creation are still viable and, if not, that they can be updated appropriately.

MISTAKE PROOFING

BE PRACTICAL

Practicality is an important consideration in deciding what type of simulation to conduct, and how to carry it off successfully in a multilocation, multidisciplinary organization. Any simulation exercise requires that the actions of all participants be logged and, post-exercise, carefully reviewed to facilitate process improvements. Fortunately, technology has evolved to make all types of crisis simulations practical in-person and/or virtually, even in distributed organizations.

The purpose of drills is not only to ensure your team can carry them out; it's also to refine your plan into something that can help you real-time, in the real world you face today.

Types of Crisis Drills

Drills and simulations range from discussions and role-play that take place in one room to realistic crisis recreations involving people and equipment at one or more locations actually simulating emergency actions. Drills typically fall into one of three categories:

Tabletop Exercises. These are scenario-driven discussions of a hypothetical emergency or crisis scenario. The discussions involve the key managers with roles in crisis or emergency response.

While the goals for "tabletops" may vary, they usually focus on identifying broad policy issues, overlapping or unassigned roles, and resource requirements.

By bringing key players together, tabletops help contribute to "team-building" in a no-fault, nonthreatening environment. If you set these up with an outside consultant who's responsible for scenario development, tabletops generally require the least client time and resources.

The exercises derive their name from the fact that they are usually conducted while participants are seated around a table in a conference or training room.

Drills. A hybrid activity falling somewhere between tabletops and full-scale exercises, drills may involve limited deployment and activation of staff and emergency personnel, again testing a hypothetical emergency or crisis scenario.

Drills may find some personnel participating in a tabletop exercise while simultaneously other response groups are deployed to the locations using the equipment that would actually be operated as part of the emergency response.

Drills may be observed and evaluated by your outside consultant or internal staff who may provide informal or formal feedback about what worked well, along with recommendations for improvement.

Drills may focus attention on certain response groups or actions; e.g., they may test the organization's emergency alert and notification capability. Drills may also be limited to certain locations or to a certain period of time (e.g., the first 24 hours after an incident occurs). Drills may also represent an opportunity for hands-on training of responders, and may be used to demonstrate whether response capabilities described on paper in crisis plans can, in reality, be executed.

Full-Scale Exercises. By definition the most complex and comprehensive, full-scale exercises as much as possible simulate the actual deployment and actions of crisis and emergency responders dealing with a hypothetical crisis scenario.

Full-scale exercises normally involve all levels of staffing, from clerical to senior managers and executives, most or all facilities that would be involved in an actual incident, and where appropriate, simulation of exercise events such as smoke, fires, or airborne releases, to name a few. Sometimes employing "actors" and "victims" playing scenario roles, full-scale exercises test most or all aspects of the client's response capabilities.

What type of simulation is right for your organization? Available resources and commitment to comprehensive preparedness are two

SMART

GET APPROVAL

MANAGING

While you may have an avid interest in getting your organization prepared for a crisis, and that's a laudatory thing, you need to be careful about how you handle crisis-related drills. It's highly unlikely that your senior management—or, if you're an outside consultant, your client—will appreciate your launching a "mock drill" without informing anyone. Don't be the boy (or girl) who cries wolf and brings the company's operations to a stop just to make a point. Bad idea.

Always ensure that whatever drills you want to conduct have the approval of senior management.

At the same time, encourage management to allow such things at inopportune times. Crises don't only happen during the 40-hour work week. They happen at night. They happen on the weekend. Keep that in mind when planning your drills.

important considerations in answering this question. The more complex the simulation and the broader its goals, the more complex and costly the simulation will be. Short of waiting for an actual crisis, simulations represent the best way to evaluate organizational preparedness while there is still time to address needed improvements. The stakes are too high to not adequately evaluate response capabilities before the crisis.

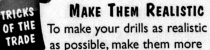

TRICKS OF THE TRADE

MAKE THEM REALISTIC
To make your drills as realistic as possible, make them more than simplistic scenarios. Don't make them simple to make your plan look good. Complicate them. Duplicate reality by having things go progressively wrong. Introduce new elements to the crisis to simulate facts changing over time. In fact, as is the case in the real world, you won't have all the information up-front, so introduce new information during the drill and test your ability to deal with it.

Drills and the Media

Practice makes ... better.

I'd love to be able to tell you that when it comes to media interview skills, "practice makes perfect," but that would be disingenuous. No amount of practice will make you a "perfect" interview subject; similarly, one or two days of media training, alone, will not leave you with lasting skills in this area unless you practice them on your own.

Some job descriptions (e.g., politician, celebrity, Fortune 100 CEO) have a lot of real-life interview practice built in. Those individuals and subordinate spokespersons are going to get plenty of opportunities to refine their skills via actual interviews.

But most of the people I've trained aren't in those kinds of jobs; instead, they are designated spokespersons who may not have to handle a really hard media interview for years after their initial training.

This is no reflection on their performance in their assigned field. The reality of dealing with the media is that it's counterintuitive to the way most of us handle interpersonal contacts. But just like a police officer who may never have to shoot a suspect for years after going through the police academy, spokespersons still have to maintain their skills so that when they're needed, they're intuitively available.

Methods of Practice

Here are ways to practice your media training skills to ensure you're ready for when a crisis breaks.

- Simulate a situation/scenario that, realistically, could occur to you/your organization.
- Simulate one or more of the types of interviews.
- Include some method of recording and playing back performance for self- or peer-critique.

There are a wide variety of ways to simulate interviews realistically enough for spokespersons to practice and improve their skills. These include:

- **Re-Enact Media Training.** Recreate the conditions under which you were media trained (e.g., tripod-mounted video camera of at least moderately high quality, someone to operate the camera, someone to play interviewer).
- **Practice "Phoner" Interviews.** Let yourself be interviewed by telephone, which is the most likely scenario for most interviews, with video becoming increasingly likely when a crisis is particularly newsworthy.
- **Staff Meeting Practices.** Take 15–30 minutes at a staff meeting and put

one or more spokespersons on the spot, with other staff members playing the role of media at a press conference.

■ **Webcam-Based Practice.** You don't have to have a media trainer return for a full training session to just get some "brush up" practice period-ically. Instead, hook up with him/her for an hour or two by Webcam periodically. That's not only useful for routine practice, but also for spot practice right before you have to give an important interview.

I've trained countless executives who claimed to have been trained in the past, but who never practiced. Most of the time, their skills were little better than the novice trainee, and sometimes what they did remember was so out of context that they actually did worse than if they had remembered nothing at all about their past training.

Make ongoing media training for your potential spokespersons part of your ongoing crisis drill training.

No, it won't make your spokespersons perfect, but it sure as heck will make them a better spokesperson.

Manager's Checklist for Chapter 5

☑ Training is not enough. If you want your crisis plan to work, practice it.

☑ Drills and simulations not only help your team perfect their crisis roles, they help identify weaknesses in your plan.

☑ There are different ways to drill, based on your needs and resources.

☑ If your role is to face the media in a crisis, practice. Then practice again. Trust me, you can't overdo it.

Crisis Response

Since there are different types of crises that can impact an organization—i.e., creeping crises, slow-burn crises, or sudden crises—there's no hard-and-fast rule about when to trigger implementation of your crisis plan and initiate crisis response.

In some circumstances it's better to "get the bad news out as soon as possible" (taking legal considerations into account). This puts you in the advantageous position of framing the story rather than letting the media—or your opposition if it's that kind of crisis—do that for you.

In other circumstances, especially the slow-burn type, you may want to take a wait-and-see approach. Sometimes a negative story will appear in one or even a few media outlets and then disappear without gaining any traction; in other words, without being picked up by other media. In those cases you *don't* want to throw fuel on the fire by overreacting; all you'll do is call more attention to the issue. It can be stressful, watching and waiting, but sometimes it's the right way to go.

Of course, there are also circumstances when the decision of whether or not to initiate crisis response isn't yours. When a sudden crisis hits—a disaster, a major accident, or say a fire destroys one of your facilities—you'll need to go into "crisis mode" immediately.

This is where all the planning, training, drilling, and holding state-

KEY TERMS

Killing the story The scenario goes like this. You get a call from a reporter telling you they're working on a story that you realize is potentially damaging. They're doing their job and asking you for comment. You ask if you can call them back, convene your core crisis team to determine what to do, what to say, etc. Someone in the group, typically a vice president with no media experience, pounds the desk and says, "They can't print that. It's not true!" or "Don't they realize they can ruin our business? You have to kill the story." Everyone at the meeting nods and agrees that the best course of action is for you to kill the media story.

Good luck with that. Unless your father- or mother-in-law happens to be the publisher of the paper or owner of the TV station where the reporter works, you're probably not going to get anywhere with that strategy.

And you can't blame the reporter for that. In fact, you ought to be grateful he or she even bothered to call you for comment in the first place. (They don't always nowdays, even though journalistic ethics say they should.)

Trying to "kill" a story in the sensationalistic journalism environment of today is largely a futile effort. Yes, you may manage it once or twice in your career as a crisis manager. But to depend on that as a crisis response tactic is, well, stupid, and only shows that the person recommending such a tactic has no clue how the media works in today's world.

Fixing the story Rather than trying to kill a story, there are ways to "fix" a story once it's been published. You can ask for, or even demand, a correction of some error of fact. In the old days (pre-Internet) this was the only kind of correction you could get. You couldn't get a publication to "correct" the "slant" of their article; sorry, that was seen by most media as intruding on their right of free speech.

Nowdays, ironically, because changing what a publication publishes online causes them no expense (they don't have to devote space to the correction), they're more likely to agree to change something you seriously object to. It's not guaranteed, but it's possible. And that's a good thing because once something is online it stays there forever. So if you have a chance to do so, take advantage of "fixing" something online. It may seem like a small success now, but it will pay off in the long run, as there will be less chance of somebody doing a search two or five years from now coming across something online that damages your organization.

ment work finally pays off. And it pays huge dividends in that you don't waste time (and money) trying to play catch-up.

But it's important to remember that when you *aren't* facing a sudden crisis, the timing of your crisis response is up to your core crisis team. So exercise judgment.

The Five Tenets of Crisis Communications

There are general principles on which you should build your crisis response, both your actions and your messages. I call them the "Five Tenets" and it's been proven over and over that they must be the mainstays of your crisis response—for the simple reason that they work.

Your crisis response must be:

Prompt. When a sudden crisis breaks that threatens or could threaten to harm people or property, seriously interrupt business, damage reputation, and/or negatively impact share value, your response must be prompt. A crisis abhors an information vacuum. If you don't communicate, rumor and innuendo will fill the void.

Compassionate. Consider the reality that addressing feelings is often more important, initially, than addressing facts. Yes, you want to get the facts out, but your response should not be totally fact-based. In crises, especially where people have been or could be harmed, your actions and messages must reflect that you actually care. If they don't, you run the risk of being cast into the league of someone who, say, runs a company that has fouled the environment on a massive scale and destroyed thousands of livelihoods but, "wants his life back" because he's tired of dealing with the consequences of what his company did.

People will forgive you if you screw up, if you show you care that you did and want to make it right. Be compassionate and communicate that.

Honest. I talk in the next chapter on "messaging" about being honest. The point here being, in your crisis response, be honest. If you're not, it may not only come back and bite you down the road, it could do so much sooner than you think.

Informative. Obviously you don't want to reveal anything that compromises your legal position. But in your crisis response you must be as informative as you can. In a crisis where people's lives, safety, or security (of any kind) are under threat, they don't want to see you stonewall. They are scared or concerned. They want answers. They want to know how this crisis affects them. If you don't tell them, somebody else will, and often they'll get it completely wrong. So, to the degree you can without jeopardizing your legal position, be forthright with information.

Interactive. Meaning, allowing two-way communication with all important audiences, using methods most appropriate to each. This is the area where I typically get the most resistance from client companies and organizations. The rationale goes, "We're telling them what they need to know. What else do they want?" What they want is an opportunity to express themselves. To vent. To offer suggestions.

An organization's crisis doesn't only happen to the organization; it also happens to its stakeholders. An organization in a crisis that shows it's willing to listen to its stakeholders takes a major step forward in winning the cooperation and loyalty of those stakeholders.

TRICKS OF THE TRADE

THE THREE CS OF CREDIBILITY

There's more to effective crisis response than verbal communications. There are also nonverbal communications.

During a crisis, effective spokespersons must, mostly through their nonverbal cues, leave audiences with the impression that they are compassionate, competent, and confident; what I call "The Three Cs of Credibility."

Think Rudy Giuliani on and after 9-11. It was his attitude, his nonverbal cues, that gave his audiences comfort. If he had delivered the same messages in a stereotypical governmental manner, the amount of fear and anxiety felt by listeners would have been dramatically higher. Instead, what they clearly felt, for the most part, was "However horrible this situation is, Mayor Giuliani is going to get us through it. He's doing the right thing, in the right way." He actually delivered little substance, initially, because so little was known. But he won over his audience.

If stakeholders perceive you as compassionate, competent, and confident, they're far more likely to believe your messages. In fact, if you're really good at projecting the "Three Cs," you can get away with some messaging errors and still win over your audience.

External Communications—The Media

As I've said elsewhere, it can seem in the midst of a crisis that the media is your most important audience. After all, the phone is ringing off the hook with requests for comments or interviews, e-mails are flying, and reporters may be camping out on your front door.

Whether they're actually your most important audience or not, you want to manage them. Nobody wants bad publicity or negative news coverage as the result of a crisis.

The old saying that "There's no such thing as bad PR" is a relic from the 20th century and was, in fact, coined by a Hollywood publicist looking to get any sort of coverage for their client. In the real world you don't want bad PR for your organization.

So how do you handle the media in a crisis? Go back to what I've mentioned before: Have holding statements that will, hopefully, give you the breathing room you need to collect the facts that you can make public.

What do you do then?

Determine how to issue the information you can. There are a number of options:

- A news release (the old term was "press release" when most media were newspapers and printed on presses), issued through a paid news service like PRNewswire or BusinessWire
- A news release issued to an in-house list of specific journalists
- A news conference (only to be undertaken when absolutely necessary as they can devolve into media "feeding frenzies"
- Interviews arranged based on the demands of the media looking to talk to you
- An exclusive interview with the most influential media outlet covering the story

Judgment comes into play here. But the goal should always be "what is the tactic that will be most effective in reaching and reassuring our stakeholders?"

Unless you're a really small organization with a very limited budget, don't make price part of the decision. Saving a few bucks but having a less effective response will cost you a lot more in the long run.

In making your decisions, be cognizant of who the media really are. The people calling you for interviews or camping out outside aren't actually stakeholders of your organizations; they're only a channel through which you can reach your stakeholders, especially the general public. Even then, the media are exactly what they claim to be—media—channels of communication. They have no investment in your organization, and you owe them nothing, much as they might like to pretend otherwise.

Some Challenges in Dealing with the Media

Remembering these sometimes-frustrating realities will help keep you out of trouble with inquiring minds that want to know. These don't describe the interaction with all reporters, but in a crisis situation you're safer if you assume they're true every time.

A reporter has the right to challenge anything you say or write, but will bristle when you try to do the same to them.

A reporter can put words in a naive source's mouth via leading questions ("Would you say that ...?" "Do you agree that ...?" "Do you feel that ... ?") and then swear by the authenticity of those quotes.

The media will report every charge filed in a criminal or civil case, with coverage focusing far more on the allegations than on responses by a defendant.

The media usually carries a bigger stick than you through its ability to selectively report facts and characterize responses, based on the public perception that "if I saw it in/on the news, it must be true."

"Off the record" often isn't, and "no comment" means "I've done something wrong and don't want to talk about it."

When the Media Go Too Far

Everyone expects journalists to be pushy, to report facts less-than-accurately at times, and to insist on a level of access to information that makes both attorneys and crisis managers cringe. To a significant extent, that's their job and those of us who respond to the media "dance the dance" with them and hope for some balance in the resulting coverage. Sometimes, however, reporters and/or the media outlet they serve go too far. They cross the line from aggressive to offensive. They insist on publishing facts that have already been corrected by reputable sources. And when they do, there is no recourse other than just taking it in the teeth.

When Reporters Get Offensive

In an actual situation that occurred to one of my clients, a reporter for an Arizona newspaper, assigned to coverage of an ongoing business crisis situation, apparently got frustrated at his inability to obtain interviews with certain representatives of that business. The organization in crisis had decided, at that point, to communicate only by written statement. The frustrated journalist called the administrative assistant to one of the business' outside attorneys and insisted on talking to the attorney. When she, appropriately, told him the "party line" that all media calls were to go to the PR director of the business (where he'd already called without success), he threatened her. He said that he would publish her name as the one responsible for information not being available to the public.

She contacted the business's crisis management consultant, who advised her boss, the attorney, that the reporter was in gross violation of journalistic ethics and advised him to write a letter explaining what had happened to legal counsel for the paper. He did and, after some communication back and forth, the paper not only apologized to the assistant in writing, but gave her a free subscription, and the reporter became the subject of an internal investigation. His bullying tactics stopped.

ETHICS LOOKUP

If you want some guidelines to help you determine if a journalist is being unethical, read the Society of Professional Journalists' Code of Ethics at spj.org/ethics_code.asp.

TOOLS

When the Media Ignore the Facts

If a spokesperson for an organization in crisis has repeatedly communicated demonstrably accurate information to the media only to see it not used, or has made statements that are repeatedly misquoted, the same tactic of having legal counsel communicate with media legal counsel can often make a positive difference. Usually, first, you want to establish a trail of evidence that you have, in fact, taken every reasonable action to get the facts corrected. You've sent polite written corrections to the reporter(s) involved. You've met with him/her in person to explain your perception of the problems. You've met with his or her supervising editor. And the problem persists.

If a media outlet's editorial bias is so strong that it won't cooperate even if threatened with more formal legal action, it's time to remember that the media is not your most important audience. Remember: We're not at the mercy of the press as much as some members of the press would like us to believe. And at its core, "the media" are people like you and I. People in every profession break the rules; they violate the ethics and responsible business practices to which they allegedly subscribe. Reporters and editors are no different. And not only do we have ways to respond but, if we don't, we're tacitly encouraging the rule-breaking.

External Communications—Beyond the Media

I write elsewhere in this book (especially in Chapter 9) about the ways the Internet has increased the challenges to effective crisis management. But it's also done something nobody expected: It's created an environment where organizations in crisis can communicate with their audiences directly.

This is, honestly, revolutionary, at least in the realm of crisis management. Thirty years ago the only ways to speak to your stakeholder audiences were (a) through the media, (b) by letter or maybe fax, and (c) via phone calls. Obviously trying to use the media was the most cost-effective method.

Today, because of the Internet, crisis managers can speak directly to their stakeholder audiences through their website, or through news releases that are posted online verbatim, or through e-mails, etc.

Technology has undercut the monopoly the media used to have on the means of communication.

Alternatives to Communicating Through the Media

Here's a list of ways to get "around" the media in your crisis situation:

- Use the Web. Either add pages to your organization's website addressing the issue, or create an entirely separate site to do so.
- Publish news releases, Q&A docs, etc., on online directories, so that those who search online for the subject can see your position as well as your position as skewed by traditional media.
- Speak directly to your stakeholders through e-mail. It's a faster, cheaper, and more effective way than we had in the past.

In addition, consider whether the audiences important to you or your client are actually being negatively influenced by the media coverage. Is it their primary source of information on the subject? I've known of cases where, when asked, key audiences have told client companies that they didn't believe the media coverage and thought reporters were on a witch hunt. It could well be that, by simply increasing positive and accurate direct communication with key audience members about a crisis situation, you'll balance out the inaccurate negativity in the press.

The Forgotten Stakeholders—Internal Communication

How many public relations spokespersons does your company have? The correct answer is "as many employees as we have." Sure, any organization can and should have a policy whereby only certain individuals are "officially" authorized to speak for the record. If a reporter calls and you have a designated spokesperson policy, the call will probably be routed correctly, but that doesn't prevent your secretary, an intern, or a junior executive from giving their version of the facts to family members, friends, PTA members, golfing buddies, and anyone else they know. Internal audiences are as, if not more important than external audiences during a crisis, and yet those who aren't actually on the crisis response team often receive the least consideration when the stuff hits the fan. It's vital, during the crisis communications planning process, to formulate key messages not only for employees, but also for others who are close enough to the organization to be considered "internal"; e.g., regular consultants and major vendors. They're the ones who are going to be asked first, by external audiences (including reporters, when they try to go around you), "What's going on?"

Here are some tips for preparing internal audiences to be an asset to crisis response:

1. **Develop one to three key messages** about the situation that are simple enough for everyone to understand, remember, and use in their day-to-day affairs. In an extremely sensitive situation, messages might be nothing more than reassuring statements and "nice no comments"; e.g., "Our day-to-day business is completely unaffected by this," "We know this is going to come out well for us when all the facts are known," or "We're a damn good company and I'm proud to work here."

2. **Brief all employees in person** about what's happening and keep them informed on a regular basis. In-person briefings say, "We care

about you," in a manner that no memo or internal newsletter can accomplish, although sometimes written communications are the only option. And you don't want internal audiences to read facts, or alleged facts, in your local newspaper first!

3. **Create a rumor-control system.** Provide means by which internal audiences can ask questions and get rapid responses. You can designate certain trusted individuals (white- and blue-collar) as "rumor control reps" who will field questions and then obtain answers from someone on the official crisis response team. And it's important to also have an anonymous means of asking questions, such as a locked drop box combined with a bulletin board on which answers to anonymous questions are posted. All employees can be encouraged to use either communication method without fear of reprisal.

Successful implementation of an internal communications program will carry your key message better, longer, and farther than most external communications, while a lack of internal communications can completely undermine even the best external strategy. The two can, and must, go hand-in-hand.

SMART MANAGING

SELF-CREATED CRISIS AND ITS MANAGEMENT

If you're causing your own crisis, that is, taking an action that has the potential of a negative reaction from stakeholders, be sure to plan to effectively:

- **Communicate internally and externally.** Remember that every employee and, often, dedicated contractors are public relations representatives and crisis managers for your organization, whether you want them to be or not. You must empower them with reassuring messages about the crisis suitable for use at their respective levels of the company. And, you don't want them to learn of the crisis from external sources before they hear about it from you.
- **Focus special communications on the most impacted customers and stakeholders.** In this age of the Internet, and in a litigious society, a few angry people can make waves completely disproportionate to their numbers or even to the injury suffered (if any). The process should include an "Escalated Cases" team to focus on such complaints when they're received.

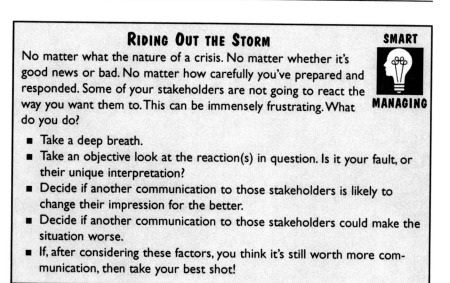

RIDING OUT THE STORM

SMART

No matter what the nature of a crisis. No matter whether it's good news or bad. No matter how carefully you've prepared and responded. Some of your stakeholders are not going to react the way you want them to. This can be immensely frustrating. What do you do?

MANAGING

- Take a deep breath.
- Take an objective look at the reaction(s) in question. Is it your fault, or their unique interpretation?
- Decide if another communication to those stakeholders is likely to change their impression for the better.
- Decide if another communication to those stakeholders could make the situation worse.
- If, after considering these factors, you think it's still worth more communication, then take your best shot!

Manager's Checklist for Chapter 6

☑ Unless it's in response to a sudden crisis, launching crisis response is a judgment call.

☑ Always follow the Five Tenets of crisis communications.

☑ In a crisis, you need to manage the media.

☑ Sometimes you don't even need the media in order to reach your most important audiences.

☑ Never forget internal communications. Your employees are your best crisis managers.

Crisis Messaging

I t doesn't matter how well thought out your crisis plan is, or how often you and your crisis response team have conducted drills or practiced potential crisis scenarios, if your crisis messaging is ineffective, it's all been for naught. Why? Because the only thing the public and your stakeholders actually see or hear are your messages.

And frankly, they don't care how much time and resources you've invested in crisis preparedness. They want to see and hear what you are doing about the problem *now.*

Hopefully, as part of your crisis planning, you've already developed crisis messages that can serve you well through a variety of crises. But the reality is there are so many potential crises that can hit an organization there is no way to develop messages before the fact that will serve in every instance. So you need to know how to create effective crisis messages in the midst of the storm.

I'm assuming you've already read Chapter 6 on crisis response and now understand the need (and value) of holding statements. Holding statements are what you say when you don't have very much to say, either because you don't have enough information to respond to questions, or you're still waiting for your organization's management and legal department to agree on what you can say publicly.

Holding statements are important because they allow you to not comment without saying "no comment." Nowadays, anyone who says "no comment" in a crisis situation is asking for trouble. The phrase is so identified with governmental bureaucrats trying to cover up corruption or crime syndicate bosses leaving a courtroom with their arm over their face that the most unsophisticated member of the general public who hears you say it knows you're covering something up.

That's why today so often in news coverage the person the media wants to talk to is "not available for comment." So they don't have to go on camera or in front of a reporter and say, "No comment."

The problem is that being unavailable for comment and not taking questions from reporters usually doesn't help you manage a crisis. If the crisis is impacting you, it's impacting your stakeholders. And presumably you *care* about its impact on your stakeholders. Why would you pass up

---

FOR EXAMPLE

UNPURE PROBLEM

Background: A crisis client was an industry trade association. A governmental agency (we'll use a fictional name like the National Governmental Agency, or NGA) had conducted a study of the industry's product, and was about to announce it had found evidence of carcinogenic activity (English: causes cancer). The problem was the NGA had studied an unpurified form of the product. That's not what the industry sold. The industry had long known the product needed to be purified. But needless to say it was concerned that the NGA report would smear the purified as well as the unpurified form of the product.

Here are the key messages we developed to use in managing the crisis:

The NGA study is grossly misleading as it analyzes an unpurified form of (the product) that members of (the product) industry do not sell.

This Association is aware of no research that indicates any risk associated with purified forms of (the product) versus the unpurified (product) that was analyzed by the NGA.

The scientific experts in (the product) industry have known for years that (the product) should be purified, which is why the Association established strict purification standards years ago.

All we're asking is that the NGA do what it has always done, which is properly distinguish between what it studied and what is commonly produced by the industry and used by consumers.

We look forward to the NGA acknowledging that the unpurified (product) they studied bears no resemblance to the purified (product) commonly used by consumers.

an opportunity to reassure them? A holding statement may not do much, but it does something, even if all it does is let your stakeholders know you care about them and you're working the problem.

The next step is developing your Key Messages.

Messaging—General Guidelines

Develop Key Messages

With holding statements available as a starting point, the crisis response team must develop crisis-specific messages required for any given stakeholder group. The team already knows, categorically, what type of information its stakeholders are looking for. What should those stakeholders know about *this* crisis? Keep it simple and manageable. Have no more than a handful of main messages for all stakeholders and, as necessary, some audience-specific messages for individual groups of stakeholders.

Don't Be Clever

Most crises have the potential to negatively impact your stakeholders and/or the general public. This is not the time to be clever. In early 2011, a fast-food company was accused in a lawsuit of having only 35 percent or so beef in one of its "beef" offerings. The company responded with an ad campaign under the headline "Thank you for suing us."

Of course a headline like that will cut through the clutter and get noticed, but everyone on the planet knows companies don't want to be sued over the quality of their products, so a response like that could be seen as either arrogant or frivolous, depending on your point of view. It certainly didn't reassure the company's customers.

Wait a minute. You're *glad* you're being sued over the quality of your product?

Use Facts, Not Fluff

In a crisis you can't get away with BS. For instance, in the same company's news release response, it said the company "prides itself on serving high quality food with great value. We're happy that the millions of customers we serve every week agree." It was nice that they reminded us their food was cheap and they were successful, but it didn't address the issue, which was the quality of their "offering." Nowadays consumers are sophisticated enough to know that having "millions of customers" doesn't mean you haven't been misleading them.

Put Things into Context

Many journalists avoid context like the plague because it tends to make their news less, well, newsworthy. That's why you should use it in your messaging when you can. If the context you provide is valid, you can change perceptions and maybe even the discussion. In this example, do other fast-food restaurants use 100 percent beef? That's something the company should have known, and if not they should have considered broadening the discussion. It's tough to pick on a company for doing what everyone else in their industry does.

CAUTION

MISTAKES AREN'T BAD, LYING IS

Don't lie in your crisis messaging. Yes, that might seem to be a given, but you'd be surprised how often it's suggested, usually by an executive who knows nothing about crisis management and is desperate to save his or her organization's reputation.

The real problem with lying isn't that it's wrong—which of course it is—the real problem is it's not worth the risk. In a crisis—at least one that's risen to the level of public attention—your organization is put in the spotlight. Maybe not all eyes, but a lot of eyes, are on you. People are watching. Your *stakeholders* are watching. Even more important, the *media* are watching. How you respond—what you say and what you do—will determine how you're judged.

If your crisis response isn't truthful, and that is discovered (and there's a good chance it will be discovered since the media will be checking out what you say) the consequences can be far more damaging, even devastating, compared to the original crisis.

People can understand if you make a mistake, and they forgive you for it. They're much less likely to forgive you for lying about it.

Give Your Messages the Smell Test

If someone claims that your product isn't 100 percent something, don't come back with the response that at least it's 88 percent of what it's supposed to be. Put yourself in the mind of your audience. When you're developing crisis messages, actually listen to your messages. Say them out loud. Pass them back and forth with your team (or if you have no team, then with other members of the organization whose judgment you

---

No Spinmeisters Needed

SMART

Don't spin in your crisis messaging. Spinning is loosely defined as twisting and turning (like spinning yarn) to give an intended interpretation. I call it "using words to obfuscate the truth." To use it in a sentence: "The spokesperson had to spin the story to make **MANAGING** it less embarrassing." Maybe 50 years ago such tactics worked; today stakeholders, including the general public, are far more sophisticated about these things.

Make sure all your messages pass the smell test. Are they not only honest and straightforward, but do they *sound* honest and straightforward?

It always amuses me when someone refers to a crisis manager as a "spin doctor." It's simply not the case. Look at the Five Tenets again (Chapter 6). You'll see the word "honest" stated outright, and clearly the theme of truthfulness runs through all five. In a crisis, it's the best policy.

---

trust). If you were one of your customers or stakeholders, would your messages work? Would they allay your concerns? If not, you have more thinking to do.

Make Your Messages Simple. Really Simple

Today most people experience the news and communications from others the way they experience speed dating—they don't spend a lot of time on any one story or message. If you want them to "get" your messages, make them simple. Really simple.

Emphasize Your Basic Message

TRICKS OF THE TRADE

Don't come up with a long list of "key" messages. First, if you have a long list of them, none of your spokespeople will be able to remember them all. More importantly, a lot of messages will cause your messaging to lose focus. Ideally you have one, basic message: either you did wrong and here's how you're going to make sure it doesn't happen again, or you didn't do wrong and here's why. All other messaging should flow from or support your basic message. It also helps if that basic message is credible and convincing.

Messaging—Specific Guidelines

Craft Your Messages for Your Audience

Remember that different stakeholder audiences may need different messages. Your supply chain partners want to know if you're still going to be able to deliver or receive shipments; they don't particularly care what steps you're taking to reassure your employees. Likewise, your employees want to know if the crisis is going to affect their jobs. They may care if you can keep shipping and receiving, but it's not their main concern.

Time Your Messaging Appropriately

Be careful not to issue messages before they're needed. You could end up unnecessarily raising concerns with a stakeholder audience and amplifying the effects of the crisis. In the example I give in the sidebar about the trade association facing an announcement by a governmental agency, it would have been foolish for us to issue our opposition to the governmental study prior to it becoming public, or even prior to it gaining any traction. "Let sleeping dogs lie" is a good old saw that applies to crisis management. At the same time, it's smart to be prepared so when the dog wakes up you know what to do.

If You Can't Issue an Understandable Message, Don't Issue One at All

Don't use language your audience doesn't understand. Jargon and arcane acronyms are but two of the ways you can be sure to confuse your audiences, a surefire way to make most crises worse. Check out a few of these taken-from-real-situations gems:

- I'm proud that my business is ISO 9000 certified.
- The rate went up 10 basis points.
- We're considering development of an SNFF or a CCRC.
- We ask that you submit exculpatory evidence to the grand jury.
- The material has less than 0.65 ppm benzene as measured by the TCLP.

Don't Issue Only Written Statements

Let's face it; it's a lot easier to communicate via written statements only. No fear of looking or sounding foolish. Less chance of being misquoted.

The problem is such an approach is impersonal and many people will think you're doing it because you're afraid. In a crisis, you don't want to appear afraid.

Use Communications Channels Appropriately

When crafting messages for your various stakeholder audiences, craft them in a way that fits the medium you're using. YouTube is not the place for a position paper. Your legal response to a lawsuit is not appropriate for a print ad in the newspaper. And most of us don't get as much TV time as Ross Perot did, so spare TV reporters your charts and graphs.

The right approach is to take your key messages and shape them into a usable form for each medium: TV, radio, print, news website, blogger, etc. And do the work in advance for the various media, so they don't have to. They'll be much more likely to use what you give them.

Manager's Checklist for Chapter 7

☑ Crisis messaging is where the rubber meets the road. Despite all you've done before, this is what your stakeholders will see and hear.

☑ When it comes to messaging, keep it real. Lying is not only wrong but dangerous, and spin is at best a waste of time and at worst counter-productive.

☑ Keep your list of key messages short. That's what "key" means.

☑ Don't waste stakeholders' time with messages not meant for them.

☑ Craft your messages to fit with the applicable communications channel.

Crisis
Recovery

Y ou've weathered the storm, now what?

The key to an organization surviving a crisis is having a well-thought-out, well-tested, and well-executed crisis plan. If you have just gone through a crisis and had a plan, great, you probably came through it with minimal damage. If you didn't have one, you probably have a lot more work to do to recover from what happened.

The reality is that all crises cause damage to one degree or another. Damage to employee morale, to customer loyalty, to market share, to stakeholder value, or some other knock against the organization. The best you can hope for is to minimize the damage. The term is, after all, Crisis Management, not Crisis Miracles.

It's been proven again and again: Organizations that prepare themselves for a crisis have a higher survival rate, and recover faster and easier than those that don't. So please follow the advice I've provided in the previous chapters. But if you weren't prepared, it's still possible to recover the position you were in pre-crisis. It may take time, but it's possible.

The way most organizations, unfortunately, attempt to recover from a crisis is to stay the course. Pretend the crisis never happened. Don't change anything. This option is taken by more organizations than you might think. They convince themselves that the crisis was an aberration, and having

Crisis recovery The actions and communications undertaken by a

KEY TERM company or organization to recover the losses caused by a crisis; such losses can be to image or reputation, goodwill, employee morale, customer loyalty, market share, or shareholder value.

gotten through it they can now "get back to business" while blithely ignoring the lessons inherent in the crisis.

At the other extreme are organizations that overreact to the challenge of the crisis. I've seen overreactions such as a recommendation to change the organization's name in order to jettison the weight of any "bad PR" associated with that name into the future. The problem with such an approach is that by changing its name, the organization is also jettisoning any remaining goodwill, brand identification, or other perceptional assets it still has. Besides, do such tactics really fool anyone?

Another overreaction is throwing money at the problem. Say your CEO gets drunk and is involved in a fatal car accident. Once the news coverage is over, a member of your board of directors suggests making a $100,000 donation to Mothers Against Drunk Drivers. Nobody else on the board is going to argue against giving money to MADD. The contribution is approved and delivered. You issue a news release. No doubt MADD is

CAUTION

IT'S NOT JUST A PR PROBLEM

Once a crisis has passed, it's not unusual for a CEO or other senior manager to react emotionally and insist you "fix our PR problem." But you can't PR your way out of a problem you behaved yourself into. Be on guard against such emotionalism. Often, a dramatic public gesture of some kind can actually further degrade the organization's image or reputation, if it is seen by the public for what it is—a cynical effort to fix your PR problem. Recommend caution, and suggest that the organization follow the rational steps outlined here.

pleased to get the donation, but nobody else cares. Your stakeholders will still have questions about the character of your leadership no matter how much money you throw at a nonprofit. In fact, the more of this kind of thing you do, the worse you look.

The rational approach to crisis recovery isn't as easy as doing nothing, and it isn't as imaginative as changing your organization's name, or as self-gratifying as giving a bunch of money to a charity and thereby expecting to buy your way out of the problem. The rational approach is to follow three essential steps, and the sooner the better.

Step One: Determine the Damage

First, use organizational resources to gauge the *actual damage* caused by the crisis. By this I mean: Don't assume

IT'S YOUR RESPONSE — **SMART**
It's important to keep in mind that often the public (and your stakeholders) will judge you more on how you handle a **MANAGING** crisis than on the crisis itself. Most of us realize people screw up, and organizations screw up. It's how they respond when they screw up—what they do and say—that leads us to draw conclusions about them. This is why the more crisis preparedness your organization does, the less crisis recovery it will have to do after the fact.

you know. Find out. Some types of damage are easy to determine; your share price falls precipitously, for instance. Or sales fall drastically and your market share takes a nosedive. Other kinds of damage, however, may not be so visible. Communicate with your stakeholders, especially your key ones. Ask them about their attitudes and perspective on both the crisis and how you handled it. This doesn't have to be a laborious process. You can do as much or as little of it as you want, but it will give you invaluable information and greatly help you determine what steps you need to take, if any, to recover from the crisis.

I say "if any" because occasionally it turns out that the *perceived damage* is not as great as the actual damage. It may appear that your reputation among the general public has been greatly tarnished, but what matters is what your stakeholders think. If they're all still behind you, happy to stay engaged with you and do business with you, you may not have to do much in the area of crisis recovery. The public, after all, has a short memory.

If, however, your relationship with your stakeholders has been damaged, *that* is something you definitely need to know so you can repair it. So find out. Again, don't assume you know. Find out for certain.

Step Two: Conduct a Post-Crisis Analysis

The second step in crisis recovery is to gauge your performance in responding to the crisis. Why is this important? So that you can fix what

DURING AND AFTER

Crisis response should always have an interactive (two-way) communication component. But that doesn't mean communicating with your stakeholders stops when a crisis is over. It's just as important to do it *after* the crisis as *during* the crisis because in order to recover from the crisis you need to know how much actual damage was done. I have seen cases (not many, but some) where great damage to a company's reputation was assumed, but when we spoke with key stakeholders afterward it turned out that wasn't the case. The company enjoyed such a high level of goodwill with its key stakeholders they were willing to overlook a single, what they considered minor, crisis.

you did wrong or any weaknesses in your crisis response process, and be better prepared next time.

Conduct a post-crisis analysis of your crisis response. If you didn't have a crisis plan, hopefully the experience you just went through convinced you that you need one. So get one done, and don't put it off.

Assuming you had a crisis plan, assemble your team and look at its performance (and the team's). Where did it hold up, and where was it weak? Where did the *team* measure up, and where are improvements needed? Draft an improvement plan to address those findings, and then make it happen.

What follows is a generic post-crisis analysis I developed in helping clients recover from crises.

POST-CRISIS ANALYSIS AND IMPROVEMENT PLAN

Date

CONTENTS

Administrative Handling Instructions	2
Executive Summary	**3**
Section 1: Situation Overview	**[P]**
Situation Details	[P]
Situation Planning Team Leadership	[P]
Participating Organizations	[P]
Section 2: Analysis of Capabilities	**[P]**
[Capability 1]	[P]
[Capability 2]	[P]
[Capability 3]	[P]

Section 3: Conclusion [P]

Appendix A: Lessons Learned [Optional] [P]

ADMINISTRATIVE HANDLING INSTRUCTIONS

The information gathered in this Post-Crisis Analysis and Improvement Plan is confidential and proprietary to (organization) and should be handled as sensitive information not to be disclosed. This document should be safeguarded, handled, transmitted, and stored in accordance with appropriate legal directives. Reproduction of this document, in whole or in part, without prior approval from (organization), is prohibited.

At a minimum, the attached materials will be disseminated only on a need-to-know basis and when unattended, will be stored in a locked container or area offering sufficient protection against theft, compromise, inadvertent access, and unauthorized disclosure.

EXECUTIVE SUMMARY

The purpose of this report is to analyze the results of (organization)'s crisis response, identify strengths to be maintained and built upon, identify potential areas for further improvement, and support development of corrective actions. It should be drafted after the Crisis Response Team has held an After-Action Conference at which the authors of this report should be identified.

This section should summarize what has occurred and answer the basic interrogatives of "Who, What, Why, When, Where, and How." Situation-specific questions that should be answered in summary include:

- What happened?
- Why did it happen?
- When did it happen?
- Where did it happen (to include other areas affected)?
- How did it happen?
- What were the company's objectives (and why)?
- Who were the company's stakeholders?
- What tactics were employed?
- What were the results?

MAJOR STRENGTHS

In general, the major strengths and primary areas for improvement should be limited to three each to ensure the Executive Summary is high level and concise.

The major strengths identified during this situation are as follows:
- Use complete sentences to describe each major strength.
- Additional major strength
- Additional major strength

PRIMARY AREAS FOR IMPROVEMENT

Throughout the situation, several opportunities for improvement in (organization)'s ability to respond were identified. The primary areas for improvement, including recommendations, are as follows:

- Use complete sentences to state each primary area for improvement and its associated key recommendation(s).
- Additional key recommendation
- Additional key recommendation
- End this section by describing the overall response as successful or unsuccessful, and briefly explain what areas the company should focus on in subsequent, similar situations.

SECTION 1: SITUATION OVERVIEW

Information in the Situation Overview should be "structured data"—written as a list rather than in paragraph form to facilitate preparation of other parts of the Post-Crisis Analysis.

SITUATION DETAILS

Situation Name: Insert formal name of situation, which should match the name in the header.

Type of Situation: Insert the type of situation (e.g., product recall, product contamination, lawsuit).

Situation Start Date: Insert the month, day, and year that the situation began.

Situation End Date: Insert the month, day, and year that the situation ended.

Duration: Insert the total length of the situation, in days or hours, as appropriate.

Location: Insert all applicable information regarding the location of specific company offices directly impacted by the situation.

Customers: List all customers (a) directly impacted and/or (b) indirectly impacted by the situation.

Capabilities: Insert a list of the target capabilities addressed within the situation.

CRISIS TEAM LEADERSHIP

The name, job title, and summary job description of each member of the Crisis Response Team for this situation should be listed along with their role in the situation.

OFFICES AND EXTERNAL ORGANIZATIONS INVOLVED IN THIS SITUATION

[Insert a list of the individual offices and external organizations (e.g., regulators, investigating authorities) involved in addressing this situation.]

SECTION 2: ANALYSIS OF CAPABILITIES

This section of the report reviews the performance of the relevant (organization)'s capabilities (e.g., purchasing, environmental compliance, safety, internal communications, external communications, planning, training). In this section, observations are organized by capability and associated activities. The capabilities linked to the situation objectives of [full situation name] are listed below, followed by corresponding activities. Each activity is followed by related observations, which include references, analysis, and recommendations.

The following outlines the information that should be contained within each Capability section of this report. (Repeat as necessary until all relevant capabilities have been reviewed.)

CAPABILITY 1: [CAPABILITY NAME]

Capability Summary: Include a detailed overview of the capability, and a description of how the capability was performed during this situation. The exact length of this summary will depend on the scope of the situation.

Activity: Identify the activity to which the observation(s) below pertain.

Observation: Begin this section with a heading indicating whether the observation is a Strength or an Area for Improvement. A strength is an observed action, behavior, procedure, and/or practice that's worthy of recognition and special notice. Areas for improvement are those areas in which the evaluators observe that a necessary task was not performed or that a task was performed with notable problems. Following this heading, insert a short, complete sentence that describes the general observation.

1. References: List relevant plans, policies, procedures, laws, and/or regulations, or sections of these plans, policies, procedures, laws, and/or regulations. If no references apply to the observation, it is acceptable to simply list N/A or Not Applicable.
2. Name of the task and the applicable plans, policies, procedures, laws, and/or regulations and 1–2 sentences describing their relation to the task.
3. Name of the task and the applicable plans, policies, procedures, laws, and/or regulations and 1–2 sentences describing their relation to the task.
4. Name of the task and the applicable plans, policies, procedures, laws, and/or regulations and 1–2 sentences describing their relation to the task.

Analysis: The analysis section should be the most detailed section. Include a description of the behavior or actions at the core of the observation, as well as a brief description of what happened and the consequence(s) (positive or negative) of the action or behavior. If an action was performed successfully, include any relevant innovative approaches used by the situation participants. If an action wasn't performed adequately, the root causes contributing to the shortcoming must be identified.

Recommendations: Insert recommendations to address identified areas for improvement, based on the judgment and experience of the evaluation team. If the observation was identified as a strength, without corresponding recommendations, insert None.

1. Complete description of recommendation 1.
2. Complete description of recommendation 2.
3. Complete description of recommendation 3.

Continue to add more observations, references, analyses, and recommendations for each capability as necessary. Maintain numbering convention to allow for easy reference.

SECTION 3: CONCLUSION

This section is an editorial conclusion for the entire document. It provides an overall summary to the report. It should include the demonstrated capabilities, lessons learned, major recommendations, and a summary of what steps should be taken to ensure that the concluding results will help to further refine plans, policies, procedures, and training for this type of incident. Subheadings are not necessary and the level of detail in this section does not need to be as comprehensive as that in the Executive Summary.

APPENDIX A: LESSONS LEARNED

While the After-Action Report/Improvement Plan includes recommendations that support development of specific post-situation corrective actions, situations may also reveal lessons learned that can be shared with the entire company. (Organization) could maintain a Lessons Learned database as a means of sharing post-situation lessons.

The type of "Lessons Learned" information you should retain includes:

- Knowledge: Knowledge and experience, positive or negative, derived from actual incidents as well as those derived from observations and historical study of operations, training, and situations.
- Best Practices: Exemplary, peer-validated techniques, procedures, good ideas, or solutions that work and are solidly grounded in actual operations, training, and situation experience.
- Good Stories: Exemplary, but non-peer-validated initiatives that have shown success in their specific environments and that may provide useful information to other elements of (organization).

- Practice Note: A brief description of innovative practices, procedures, methods, programs, or tactics that (organization) used to adapt to changing conditions or to overcome an obstacle or challenge.

Step Three: Do a Vulnerability Audit

The third step in crisis recovery is to do what you can to avoid another crisis. This means finally doing a vulnerability audit. Just because you had a crisis over one issue doesn't mean there isn't another one looming out there ready to test you yet again—maybe as soon as tomorrow. Do an audit to see if you can head it off.

Manager's Checklist for Chapter 8

☑ You can recover from a crisis, but it's a lot easier if you followed a well-tested crisis plan.

☑ In trying to recover from a crisis, your options run the gamut from doing nothing to doing too much. Try not to fall into either trap.

☑ There are three essential steps to rational crisis recovery: determine the damage, conduct a post-crisis analysis, and do a vulnerability audit.

☑ A post-crisis analysis of your crisis response can be as simple or complex as you want. The key is addressing and correcting those factors that weren't effective.

☑ If you didn't do a vulnerability audit or create a crisis plan before your crisis—are you convinced now?

Online Reputation Management

Online Reputation Management (ORM) is the use of the Internet to defend the reputation of a company, organization, or individual. This is accomplished in two ways.

First, through monitoring what is said about the organization on the Internet through its multitude of venues and, second, through the use of the Internet to respond to these statements and offset any negative influence on stakeholders.

In today's connected world it's become the most important way a crisis manager can defend a company's reputation.

Why? Because unlike the traditional media of the past—newspapers, magazines, radio, television—the Internet directly or indirectly reaches almost everyone on earth. And it reaches them *now*.

The Impact of the Internet

The International Telecommunication Union reports that 2 billion people—a third of the world's population—are Internet users. IMS Research (a market research company in the IT industry) reports that the number of Internet-connected devices is about to pass the 5 *billion* mark. But by 2013, says global technology leader Cisco Systems, Inc., the number of connected devices will grow to *1 trillion*. That means there will be a 200-fold increase in connected devices in three years or less.

Think about that. From 1450, when Gutenberg invented movable type, it took more than 300 years for most people, even in the industrialized nations, to have access to a daily newspaper. Today there are still less than 6,500 daily newspapers in the world, selling less than 395 million copies a day. Far less reach than the Internet, which is why most newspapers now have an online edition.

Television was invented in the 1920s, yet it wasn't until the 1960s that a broadcast signal reached everyone in America, let alone the rest of the world. So, in less than 20 years, the Internet has far surpassed any other previous medium in its reach. The growth has been simply stupendous.

But the impact of the Internet is even more significant for an important reason. Nobody owns it. The reach of traditional media was always limited by the fact that its venues were owned by individual interests and restricted to individual locations. Because the owners of the *New York Times* couldn't afford to distribute it everywhere, you couldn't read the newspaper unless you subscribed to it, or it was sold on a newsstand in your town. But the Internet allows you to reach everybody in the world and receive information from everybody as long as you have a way to connect; meaning we all have access to information and messages we never had before. Instantaneously.

The world has never before seen a medium that has the potential to let everybody reach everybody at any given moment. It's a huge challenge to crisis managers seeking to defend the reputation of an organization. Why?

FOR EXAMPLE

WikiLeaks

One of the best examples of an online crisis is the WikiLeaks controversy of 2010 in which even the United States government was forced to deal with a crisis born of the Internet. The release of thousands of classified documents threatened both America's alliances and its relations with many countries. It also ruined careers and put at risk the lives of many who had worked with or for the United States. International efforts to stop the leaking were met by WikiLeaks supporters who created "mirror sites" to continue the release of secret material—an example of viral nature of Internet communications and the loyalty online activists feel to each other.

This is an extreme example of an online crisis, but it shows that no one is immune from such threats.

The I-Reporter—Born of the Web

The Internet has become the largest media outlet, additionally so with the invention of the World Wide Web (or "the Web" as everybody calls it) in the early 1990s. Interactive print, audio, and video communications are all available, with the line between "amateur" and "professional," and between "traditional" and "nontraditional" media blurred almost beyond comprehension.

This massive medium has spawned what I call "The I-Reporter," a term I coined long before CNN started using it to refer to their citizen-reporters. An I-Reporter is essentially anyone who chooses to share information publicly on the Internet, regardless of its accuracy.

What is the relevance of an I-Reporter to online reputation? Consider these realities:

Anyone with a way to connect to the Internet can be an I-Reporter. They can post anything they want anytime they want.

While some I-Reporters compete for commercial gain, others compete simply for the joy of recognition. Just as traditional media reporters want to show up on page 1 of a newspaper, or at the top of the broadcast news, many I-Reporters want their material showing up on page 1 of a Google search or on CNN's home page.

I-Reporter Anyone who chooses to share information publicly on the Internet, regardless of its **KEY TERM** accuracy. Such individuals have various motives, from commercial gain to an intent to do damage to a simple desire for recognition to an impetus for social progress. They often know a great deal about how to get high search engine placement for their postings, meaning they can have an influence online well out of proportion to their standing. Of even more concern, they rarely have journalism training or operate within the ethical guidelines traditional media reporters and editors are expected to follow.

Often I-Reporters are their own publishers and site promoters, or work in small teams to provide these functions, and know how to get better search engine placement and more attention on the Internet than "competing" entities.

Search engine ranking has very little—and sometimes nothing—to do with quality or accuracy of content.

Information posted on the Internet propagates virally—it spreads via links or reprinted pages on websites, blogs, or other online points of presence run by people of like mind. Even total misinformation is blatantly re-reported at websites operated by supposedly legitimate organizations.

Some I-Reporters are constrained by the conditions of their employer; some are constrained by a sense of ethics; but most are completely unconstrained except by law—where it can be enforced.

Throw into this cauldron of communication the fact that the general public still hasn't fully realized how easy it is to misrepresent information on the Internet. So they often believe what they read without questioning its veracity. And the witch's brew has now become a difficult environment challenging many ethical and honest organizations.

Organizations have always had individuals who disagreed with their policies, disliked their products or services, are disgruntled former employees, or had a bad experience with a receptionist. In the past, unhappy individuals could call or write letters to the company, contact the Better Business Bureau, or even seek the help of their local consumer reporter. Today, just as quickly or more so, they can complain online. And their potential reach is endless.

Crisis managers used to worry primarily about bad headlines in their local newspapers or some negative telephone feedback from their various stakeholders. Damage control was usually local or regional, and seldom did negative news reach the ears or eyes of people outside the immediate region. No more.

Today, 90 percent of the crises on which I and other crisis managers work have a significant Internet component. In many of these situations, the organization has done little or no wrong. In others, there are small truths and half-truths buried in the mountain of rumors and

KEEP MONITORING

Monitoring your online reputation is a valuable business practice. Even if you go months or years without suffering an online threat, don't fall into the trap of thinking the time and resources were wasted. When evaluating your monitoring efforts, see them for what they are: an investment in protecting your reputation. It only takes one online crisis to more than prove the value of monitoring and advance preparation.

innuendo created by what is usually a tiny number of vociferous and pro-lific Internet critics.

Comedian Jon Stewart has described the Internet as "the world pass-ing around notes in a classroom." In some ways that's true. In other ways, unfortunately, it's like the school bully being given a bullhorn.

Other Sources of Online Threats

I-Reporters are not the only source of threats to reputation on the Inter-net. In fact there are a number of possible sources. But two of the most common are threats from traditional media and threats from official and quasi-official sources.

The traditional media of newspapers, magazines, radio, and televi-sion are having a difficult time dealing with the explosion of the Internet. Accustomed to charging for access to their content (readers/viewers) or inclusion with their content (advertisers), they're challenged to find ways to cope with the Internet's generally free model of operations. While they scramble to find ways to generate revenue in return for the information they provide (as required by their business model), most traditional media outlets have chosen to make the majority of their con-tent available online. As a result, Internet users around the world can now access content from many traditional news media they didn't have access to before. And these media are often the source of potentially damaging information. The difference between today and 20 years ago is that their content is now widely available online and, therefore, to every-one. You no longer have to live in New York to read what *The New York Times* reports on an organization.

Another source of online threats that deserves special attention is official or quasi-official sources. Governmental agencies, nongovern-mental organizations (NGOs), think tanks, research firms, citizen and consumer groups—many of which possess enhanced credibility due to their nonprofit status—are now more likely to announce their findings or opinions online than through traditional media. Any organization that works in the public realm must be on guard against statements from such sources that threaten its reputation.

BAD NEWS HAS LEGS

CAUTION

With the advent of the Internet, negative news or publicity in even a small local newspaper has "legs" it never had before. Most traditional media are posting their content online as well as printing it in their publications, especially their most sensational stories. Today, if your company or organization has a crisis that would previously only matter in Florida, you can expect most people in California to soon know about it. With the Internet the geographic "containment" of crises has gone out the window. Understanding this new reality is crucial to companies and organizations with nationwide stakeholders—investors, customers, suppliers, and others. There is no such thing as strictly local news anymore.

ORM Terms

Before we talk about how crisis managers should deal with I-Reporters and other Internet threats to reputation, it's important to define some basic ORM terminology. This is important because the Internet has in many ways created its own language that crisis managers must understand if they are to mount an effective online defense of their organization.

Website. A set of interconnected Web pages, usually including a homepage, generally all located on the same server, and prepared and maintained as a collection of information by a company, organization, or person (e.g., *bernsteincrisismanagement.com*). Websites can be yours, your opponents', or a third party's.

Blog. De facto, a diary on a website; a frequently updated personal journal chronicling links at a website, intended for public viewing (e.g., *bern-*

DON'T IGNORE BLOGGERS

CAUTION

Bloggers are nothing more than individuals voicing their personal opinions, right? Wrong. Today, many are operating as full-fledged journalists (Note: Blog *means* online journal) and are followed by loyal reading publics. And research shows that the majority of traditional reporters and news editors now read blogs for story tips and background for their own stories. So don't ignore bloggers. Follow those who follow your industry, company, or organization, so that you'll know if they mention you, and can be prepared before a reporter calls to follow up on what they've posted.

Who blogs about you? You can find out by searching sites such as *technorati.com, regator.com,* or *blogsearch.google.com*.

steincrisismanagement.blogspot.com). Blogs can, like websites, be used for online communications by any party who creates them.

Wiki. A website that allows the easy creation and editing of any number of interlinked Web pages via a Web browser using a simplified markup language or a WYSIWYG (what you see is what you get) text editor. Credibility varies since virtually anyone can add content, but due to their construction Wikis can rank high in online searches. Wikipedia is one of the better Wikis, in that it has committed itself to continuous improvement monitored by an independent board of advisors.

Social Media. A type of online media designed to facilitate writer/reader interactivity and rapid communication (e.g., Facebook, LinkedIn, Twitter, MySpace). Some believe social media communications will replace traditional e-mail in the not-too-distant future.

Points of Presence (POP). Any location on the Internet where you have a presence clearly associated with your name and/or brand. POPs are your friends if you use them correctly.

Search Engine Optimization (SEO). The process of improving the ranking on a search engine (e.g., Google, Yahoo!, Bing) of any of your points of presence. The Internet is free but it's not equal. SEO can be your friend in making your case online.

Who You Gonna Call?

With the growth of the Internet, companies looking to increase business have been quick to jump on the bandwagon, and some have learned how to use it to promote their products and services, or to build brand awareness and enhance their reputation.

As a result, when an Internet-based threat to reputation emerges, these companies sometimes assume it should be dealt with by the people who built their online presence—Marketing or IT personnel.

Bad idea. While Marketing people are great at promoting organizations, they are not generally familiar with how to defend them. Likewise, many organizations have IT personnel on staff or on-call, but though their expertise is invaluable from a technical standpoint, it rarely translates into effective Internet communications when it comes to ORM.

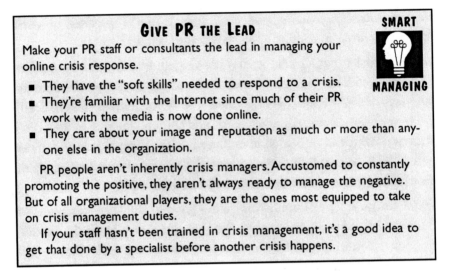

GIVE PR THE LEAD

SMART

Make your PR staff or consultants the lead in managing your online crisis response.

MANAGING

- They have the "soft skills" needed to respond to a crisis.
- They're familiar with the Internet since much of their PR work with the media is now done online.
- They care about your image and reputation as much or more than anyone else in the organization.

PR people aren't inherently crisis managers. Accustomed to constantly promoting the positive, they aren't always ready to manage the negative. But of all organizational players, they are the ones most equipped to take on crisis management duties.

If your staff hasn't been trained in crisis management, it's a good idea to get that done by a specialist before another crisis happens.

It's important to remember that the Internet is simply a medium, more effective than any other in history, but a medium nonetheless. If *TIME* magazine called for an interview, the CEO would turn to the PR department for help, not the IT department. He or she should do the same when a challenge emerges via the Internet. Better yet, he or she should have the PR department call on their crisis manager.

Examples of Online Reputation Threats

How much of a threat does the Internet actually pose to an organization? After all, with such an avalanche of information already online, isn't the impact of an online threat diminished if not completely "lost in the clutter"? Consider these real-life examples.

Thousands of members of a trade association watch their profits erode as the result of coordinated and vicious online attacks by a small handful of detractors on a personal vendetta, detractors who also knew how to get their attacks listed on the first page of a Google search.

An industry-leading financial services company finds itself on the wrong end of complaints by state Attorneys General fueled, to a great extent, by online—and highly inaccurate—reports from the Better Business Bureau. Search engine results for the company's name also motivate one insurer to deny them liability coverage.

A public school district's governing board that restricted its communication based on legal and privacy considerations gets picked apart on the Internet by a tiny group of disgruntled parents with a grudge and who are unwilling to work "within the system."

The manufacturers, distributors, and retailers of a safe health-food product are faced with the release of a research report by a governmental agency that suggests their product is unsafe because it was based on questionable science.

These are only a few of hundreds of available examples of online threats to legitimate organizations launched by a small group of opponents, or fueled by the Internet's tendency to "report" all news as though it's equally credible.

Online Reputation Management— The Strategic Side

How can an organization deal with the challenge of online threats to its reputation? First, let's look at the strategic side of the challenge.

Everything said about your organization on the Internet must be put into its proper perspective. Don't expect to have 100 percent approval all the time. Remember that just like a totally balanced traditional news story, 50 percent—at best—of "your side" of a story will be represented.

Always monitor critics to see if they either (a) draw the attention of your stakeholders and/or (b) start to achieve high search engine ranking. If so, have your crisis team meet to discuss the pros and cons of PR and legal responses that could force inaccuracies off the Web, or demonstrate to concerned stakeholders, on your own Web pages and/or through offline tactics, why they have no reason for concern.

It's impossible to completely contain a crisis once it hits the Internet. An article on a local newspaper site or a critic's blog is accessible worldwide—instantly. If the site is properly optimized, it will also show up on Internet searches using search terms important to your organization.

It has always been true that in the absence of communication, rumor and innuendo fill the gap, but the Internet ensures that the gap is filled, and grows, far more quickly. Just look at all of the Internet hoax e-mails we get, and then you can understand why those e-mails that aren't hoaxes— but aren't confirmed as the truth, either—titillate us to pass them on.

The Internet exponentially increases the prospect of confidential information being leaked. I've seen Internet critics publish not merely confidential documents, but also audio recordings of broadcast voicemail and video taken for internal use only by the target organization. Often, this information is leaked from disgruntled current or former employees. Sometimes it's obtained off inadequately protected websites.

When faced with an online threat to which a response is necessary, don't depend solely on Web-based tactics to respond. Don't always fight fire with fire; you could end up unintentionally escalating the conflict. Instead, use direct-to-stakeholder communications. Not only will this allow you to tell your side of the story, your stakeholders will appreciate hearing directly from you.

SMART
MANAGING

CHECK WHAT'S GOING ON ONLINE FIRST

You don't have to respond to every Internet critic, but you do have to monitor them closely. The best thing to do is evaluate each Web posting as it appears. What's the nature of the comment? Is it a personal complaint or does it rise to the level of an issue that may attract other supporters? If it's a personal complaint, address the poster personally, ideally via private e-mail or at one of their social media pages. Offer to and work to resolve their complaint. If it's an issue that can or has attracted supporters, evaluate it as a threat. You may still be able to address it directly. If it's quickly spinning out of control and attracting the attention of stakeholders, then you have an online crisis. Execute your crisis plan (assuming you have one).

Also, don't automatically assume you have to respond to every Internet critic. Not every Internet posting goes viral and threatens your organization. Sometimes a response can do more to spread an attack than the initial posting!

If allegations have already propagated widely and have caused considerable damage, with the possibility of worse damage ahead, consider getting more aggressive from a PR and legal perspective.

At the same time, never take legal action against hostile websites without professional consideration of the PR implications, and don't let PR actions against hostile websites be implemented without legal consideration. Your PR and legal teams must work side-by-side.

Strive to be aware of the thoughts and feelings of your stakeholders—internal and external—so that you know when and how severely Internet-centered negativity is impacting them. If you do, you will also know when they think you're doing a good job responding to such negativity.

Safeguards

So, what kind of safeguards can a smart organization put in place to avoid or cope with such challenges?

Ensure that an Internet-savvy staff person or consultant is responsible for continuous monitoring of news related to your organization and its industry. The lowest-cost (free!) means of monitoring online news and information is via Google Alerts (*google.com/alerts*), but they are not as thorough as tracking by any of the many fee-paid services. Need further motivation to do this? You can count on the fact that both your competitors and critics are already doing so!

Don't rely on others to support your organization in times of crisis. During the Mad Cow scare in the United States, the only authority figures were governmental officials who were spouting bureaucratic and scientific jargon that didn't clearly answer the most important question on the mind of any consumer, "Is my hamburger safe to eat?" Food industry officials and business leaders have told me, since then, that they were woefully unprepared to respond to staff and customers with reliable and easy-to-digest information on Mad Cow, even though a U.S. outbreak was an "it's bound to happen" threat.

Copyright everything you publish on the Internet—text, photos, video, artwork, trademarks, brand names, etc. This gives you legal and PR recourse if a critic or anyone uses your material without permission. I have an association client that successfully engaged critics who published (and in some cases ridiculed) their copyrighted materials (e.g., pictures of board members), forcing the critics to remove that information and even apologize for using it. Legal counsel was able, in some cases, to formally copyright some of the material long after it was originally published on our client's sites and critic sites, so it's never too late to submit the correct paperwork to the U.S. Copyright Office (*copyright.gov*).

COPYRIGHT YOUR STUFF

Copyright and/or trademark everything you publish on the Internet.

Copyright law states that anything you create automatically holds a copyright. That's great; try proving it in court.

Far more protective is that you've registered your copyright. You can do this at *copyright.gov*.

You should register the copyright of text, photos, video, artwork, trademarks, brand names, etc., essentially anything you put online. It's easy to do, and it protects you against others using your own material against you online (don't think it can't happen).

The best practice is: Whatever it is you put online, register your copyright and/or trademark.

Retain legal counsel that understands the growing field of Internet law. Many don't!

GET THE RIGHT ATTORNEY

If you're facing a serious enough online crisis, retain an attorney who specializes in Internet law. Many say they do but aren't really qualified. A qualified attorney can help you remove Internet postings that are libelous, without standing, or just plain inaccurate.

Why does this matter? Because almost everything on the Internet stays on there forever. If it's truly wrong, you don't want it on there. And the right attorney can help you get it off.

Where do you find an Internet-savvy attorney? While personal referrals are great when possible, you can also try the American Bar Association's Lawyer Locator at *abanet.org/lawyerlocator/searchlawyer.html*. "Internet Law" is one of the pull-down-menu specialties you can select when searching.

Dealing with Internet Critics

How do you keep from making matters worse when you're dealing with people who don't have the standards and checks and balances you're accustomed to in the mainstream media? When should you respond, and when shouldn't you? There's no single answer, but here are some things to consider:

The C-Factor. The term "Q-Factor" has become fairly well known as the measurement of a celebrity's recognition quotient. In 2005, I introduced the concept of C-Factor, *Credibility Factor*, as the measure of how believable individuals or organizations are to stakeholders for any particular issue.

Who are the most dangerous critics? A dangerous Internet critic is one who (a) has a

C-Factor The measure of how believable individuals or organizations are to stakeholders for any particular issue.

KEY TERM

high C-Factor and (b) strong SEO skills, which result in a highly ranked website or posting. Either one of these criteria, alone, can cause damage, but together they can be devastating. The critic can be providing totally or largely erroneous information, but if it "reads" credibly and is highly ranked, your stakeholders will see it, and many will believe it. In such cases, it's essential to find ways to (a) come across with a higher C-Factor at online locations of your choosing (pick your battlefield) and (b) ensure that you engage in superior SEO tactics. There's no excuse for allowing an Internet critic's site to rank higher than yours.

Timing. The best time to engage a savvy Internet critic may be as soon as he or she appears online, which requires close monitoring.

Your attitude should be one of concerned and empathetic interest, i.e., "We care very much what others think of us, we respect your right to

TAKE THEM ALL SERIOUSLY

CAUTION

Don't dismiss Internet critics because they have no standing on an issue and you assume they therefore have no credibility. All too often, today, high search engine ranking equals credibility; especially when this is coupled with information that "reads" credibly. Take every critic seriously until they've shown they are not a threat.

disagree/criticize, and would like to know what kind of information we can provide to help you understand our organization better." It won't always work, but documenting your attempts at compassionate and ethical contact will give you a paper trail useful both for PR and legal purposes, should the critic escalate efforts to damage your organization.

Education and Reorientation

A good general has, at some time, also learned how to shoot a rifle, march, and effectively engage the enemy. And a good manager has had extensive training in the wide array of skills required for his or her job. But far too many of the leaders in all types of organizations have not gone through "Internet basic training" other than having some facility with e-mail and browsing the Web. How can they be expected to engage and neutralize or defeat an opponent who's smart, fast, and isn't bogged down by bureaucracy? And who is often well networked with other guerilla-tactic critics who know how to be David to your Goliath?

Educate yourself and your organization's decision makers. Learn the jargon and tactics unique to Internet communications. Understand the environment—the battlefield, if you will—in which you're competing for credibility.

There are some scary parallels between what the U.S. military has learned while fighting in the Middle East and what's happening on the Internet, because in both cases, old, slow (more than a few hours) decision making and implementation gives terrorists—and Internet attackers—a real advantage. Most organizations aren't structured for rapid online response, but if they don't change, their C-Factor and bottom line will continue to suffer.

A colleague of mine, Gerald Baron, wrote a book on this subject whose title summarizes the challenge you face. The book is called *Now Is Too Late* (Edens Veil Media, 2006). But if you get ahead of this nasty curve, it doesn't have to be too late for your organization.

FAST RESPONSE

Be structured for rapid online response. As mentioned in previous chapters, you need a crisis team. The key here is to include on your team someone with online skills and expertise, someone who understands the Internet and how its various components work together.

But that's not all you need. You also need a fast decision-making process. With an online crisis spreading virally, you can't wait until tomorrow for a meeting to discuss how to meet the threat.

And with legal considerations usually in the forefront of any crisis response, you need a process that will expedite clearance of your crisis response with legal considerations.

The Role of SEO in Online Reputation Management

As defined above, search engine optimization (SEO) is the process of improving the ranking on a search engine (e.g., Google, Yahoo!, Bing) of any of your points of presence. Why is this important, and how can it be used in online reputation management?

With the Internet being the largest and most powerful news medium available, what do you want people to find when they search for your organization's name on Google (which has 60 percent of search traffic) or the other

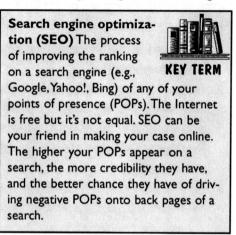

Search engine optimization (SEO) The process of improving the ranking on a search engine (e.g., Google, Yahoo!, Bing) of any of your points of presence (POPs). The Internet is free but it's not equal. SEO can be your friend in making your case online. The higher your POPs appear on a search, the more credibility they have, and the better chance they have of driving negative POPs onto back pages of a search.

KEY TERM

major search engines? You definitely don't want them to find any of the following:

- A vicious blog started by disgruntled former employees.
- Most of the links leading to websites or blogs critical of your organization.
- Websites and blogs that you don't control, while your own sites are buried on later Google pages (research shows very few Google users even look at links beyond the first two pages).
- Your organization's name prominently and negatively mentioned on legitimate (e.g., an Attorney General's office) or quasi-legitimate (RipOff Report), consumer-focused websites.
- Your organization's name connected with an investigation by any regulatory or enforcement agency.

The reality of the Internet is that you can't stop these sorts of listings from appearing on search engines. You can, however, proactively affect *where* they appear in a search by ensuring that *your* points of presence rank higher and are therefore more likely to be seen, thereby helping to defend or enhance your organization's online reputation.

Just as relatively few PR practitioners have extensive experience with crisis management, relatively few SEO practitioners understand how to engage in SEO online reputation management. One who does is Chesa Keane of Tao Consultants, Inc. She often counsels clients to follow these 10 steps.

1. Focus on Google for search results; the other search engines will follow suit over time.

2. Review your website for keyword placement and density (keyword/total word ratio); you won't be found if the keywords aren't present in the proper configuration (i.e., there are requirements for the number of keywords used in different parts of the code that creates the page).

3. Update your website frequently; stale sites drop fast and fresh information keeps your site "sticky" (viewers stay and return).

4. Present clear calls to action; give your visitor a reason to respond.

5. Validate your Web pages for error-free code; Google downgrades poorly constructed websites.

6. Content must be relevant to both the website and the Web page.

7. Avoid Flash content and overuse of JavaScript and frames pages; these websites cannot be reliably indexed by search engines.

8. Obtain inbound links from relevant, high-profile websites with good Page Rank.

9. Create multiple points of presence (e.g., blogs, article publication, activity at forums, social media), where you can get as many positive messages out as possible, pushing the negative messages down on a search engine results page.

TRICKS OF THE TRADE

FRONT-LOAD THE POSITIVE

You can't prevent negative POPs. What you can do is front-load your search engine rankings so that crisis-related or negative POPs appear on pages further back. Negative "news" or postings about your company or organization may still appear on searches, but be too far back for the average searcher to notice. How do you do this? By using solid SEO tactics. Follow Chesa Keane's 10 SEO steps for online reputation management.

10. Monitor search engines constantly and adapt quickly based on the results.

Manager's Checklist for Chapter 9

☑ The number of Internet users is huge and growing exponentially every year.

☑ The Internet is, de facto, the world's largest newspaper, one with writers who usually have no professional or ethical restraints.

☑ It's a critical management skill to have a strong awareness of the potential of the Internet for good or evil, as well as familiarity with certain Internet-related terms.

☑ Virtually all crises today have an Internet component. Many are completely Internet-driven.

☑ Rapid response is critical to effective Internet communications, and that requires advance preparation.

Crisis Management and the Law

Here's a hypothetical conversation between three members of an organization's crisis response team as they struggle to manage a crisis. In the room are the organization's staff attorney or outside legal counsel, its crisis manager, and the CEO. This scene happens all too often in the real world.

CEO: "So, what should we do?"

Attorney: "We shouldn't do anything publicly. We shouldn't issue any public statement. We'll probably be hit with hundreds of lawsuits. Whatever we say could come back to haunt us in future litigation."

Crisis Manager: "If we don't say anything we'll look guilty. We have to speak to our stakeholders—customers, employees, and the public. We'll use tactics and messages that'll show compassion and action while protecting the organization. And the sooner we do it, the better chance we have of limiting the life of the story."

Attorney: "That's just going to cause problems down the road."

Crisis Manager: "It's what we have to do."

CEO (looking from one to the other): "You two aren't helping me much."

Many crisis managers believe—whether they'll admit it openly or not—that in a crisis situation their chief obstacle to effective management often isn't the crisis itself, it's their own organization's attorney or legal team. At the same time, a lot of lawyers probably wish they never had to contend with crisis managers. Where's the disconnect? After all, both sides are supposed to be on the same team. As one crisis management specialist wrote in an article on this subject in my online newsletter, "Why can't we all just get along?"

Well, we can, and I'll get to that, but first a few words about why the disconnect happens in the first place. It's simple, really. In a crisis the crisis manager and the attorney have different goals. So naturally they are going to recommend different strategies. And management is caught in the middle.

When a crisis is brewing, and especially once it hits, the attorney's job it to protect the organization from legal threats such as lawsuits, charges of regulatory noncompliance, and others, including in severe cases possible indictment of management. His or her efforts revolve around the legal and court system. The crisis manager of course wants to protect the organization's legal position, but his or her job is primarily to defend the organization in the court of public opinion.

> **KEY TERM** **The court of public opinion** "Public opinion" is the aggregate of individual attitudes or beliefs held by the general public. "The court of public opinion" is a term used to describe public attitudes and beliefs related to a particular issue. The legal metaphor is apt because the public generally "passes judgment" on the issue after hearing testimony from both sides through both traditional and social media.

This is where cooperation can break down. As the crisis develops or breaks, the crisis manager is recommending communication, often if not primarily through the news media. And there's the rub. By its very nature communication is *discoverable,* meaning the potential exists for your communications to be used against you by a plaintiff or prosecutor.

Also, there's the media, which are not *controllable* (particularly social media), and therefore, to many attorneys, to be avoided at all costs. It's their job to protect the organization from anything that risks putting it or its management in legal jeopardy, and to many of them talking to the media falls into that category. Big time.

To a degree you can see their point. Today's sensationalist media have impacted the public environment to the degree that, regardless of the legal merits of any crisis situation, perceptions generated from case onset through resolution can be as helpful or damaging as the "provable facts." They can also affect the attitude of prosecutors, regulators, and other audiences important to the legal process.

But that's exactly why attorneys should work together with crisis managers. Well-conceived and -executed crisis management strategies and messaging can also *benefit* an organization's legal position by helping to stabilize that environment and positively impact those perceptions among vital audiences.

In the court of public opinion, failing to do so is like holding a trial with only the prosecution in the courtroom.

No Communication Is Communication

Failing to communicate during a crisis is, in the eyes of the public, an admission of guilt. In the majority of cases (unless the evidence is demonstrably otherwise), the public generally suspends forming a judgment until it has heard enough information to do so. If your organization remains silent, you essentially pass up the opportunity to speak to the public when it's at its most receptive. Point this out to your organization's decision makers. Remind them that in this instance silence is not golden. If management still defers to the legal team, work with them to craft messages along the lines of what I've outlined in the chapters on crisis response and crisis messaging. These guidelines will help you craft messages that are both effective and potentially acceptable to the legal department.

Integrating Crisis Management and Legal Strategy

I've worked with a number of attorneys over the years who understood the need to take public opinion into account when defending an organization during a crisis. Indeed, progressively more attorneys are coming to understand they shouldn't just *tolerate* crisis management, they should actively *cooperate* with it on their clients behalf.

Ed Novak, Phoenix office managing partner at the law firm of Polsinelli Shugart, whose Arizona practice includes white-collar criminal defense matters, has said that crisis management "Is particularly important during the investigatory phase because you have a greater opportunity to influence how your client is viewed by the media. You want journalists to receive a positive first impression, which hopefully will carry through the investigation. If you look like you're covering up or stonewalling, the negative impression created will be difficult to erase."

But, Novak also says, crisis management "also has distinct roles to play at the time of charging, pre-trial, and during a trial. A crisis management expert can give me an objective layperson's view of what I plan to show to a jury or prosecutor, often providing valuable criticisms or suggestions." Novak also noted that having a spokesperson other than legal counsel, one trained by a crisis management consultant, can prevent sometimes-overwhelmed attorneys from reacting inappropriately to eager reporters.

COOPERATION IS KEY

I'm arguing in this chapter for greater cooperation between attorneys and crisis managers, but it's important to note I'm *not* advocating crisis managers be given free reign without concern for legal considerations. In developing your crisis management strategies and messages, you must always defer to Legal. The key is doing this without letting the organization "play ostrich."

The best way to avoid the logjam of differing recommendations that can arise between crisis managers and attorneys is to work together *before* any crisis arises. Both parties need to understand the other's responsibilities, goals, and value to the organization in managing a crisis. Agree beforehand on the processes you'll follow in the event of a crisis: how you'll work together to cope with unexpected new developments, how new messaging and communications will be reviewed and approved when they're needed, etc.

And once a crisis breaks, don't hold any meetings about how to manage things without both sides in the room. Leaving out either perspective can lead to decisions that are one-sided and not in the organization's best interest.

Common Ground in the Legal vs. Crisis Management Debate

Here are some tactical recommendations that typically come out of legal counsel during a crisis. As a crisis manager you should agree to these. They make sense. Plus, when the attorney on your crisis response team proposes these and finds you agree, he or she may possibly be more will-

ing to go along with some of
your tactical recommenda-
tions.

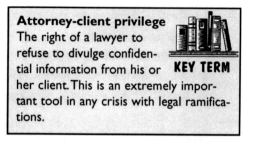

Attorney-client privilege
The right of a lawyer to
refuse to divulge confiden-
tial information from his or   **KEY TERM**
her client. This is an extremely important tool in any crisis with legal ramifica-
tions.

1. Ensure that Legal is part
   of your crisis response
   team. All actions and
   statements by the organi-
   zation in response to the crisis should be vetted by your attorney.

2. Stop employees from discussing or communicating with each other
   (and especially with nonemployees) about the crisis or issue until
   further notice. This means e-mails, internal memos, "water cooler
   chat," indeed, *any* discussion of the crisis. The reason is all these
   communications are "discoverable" and can be used against your
   organization in any future legal proceeding.

3. If discussion or communicating about the crisis must take place
   (which of course it must), make sure your legal counsel is part of the
   discussion or communication. Include your attorney on all e-mails,
   and include a message postscript explicitly stating the message is
   "attorney-client privileged." If meetings must be held, have your
   attorney present.

4. Don't destroy any documents, and if you have a regular document
   destruction process, suspend it. Until your attorney says otherwise,
   stop all shredding and other forms of document destruction. You may
   be obligated to present evidence, and since you won't know exactly
   what constitutes evidence, protect yourself by not destroying anything.

5. Back up your hard drives. This will help you maintain operations
   even if your IT system becomes subject to a search warrant or subpoena.

6. Collect all pertinent documents. If things take a legal turn, very likely
   all documents pertaining to the crisis will eventually have to be provided. Don't wait until you are ordered to provide such documents,
   which could cause a disruption to operations while staff scrambles
   to collect them. Begin pulling them together immediately, ideally
   under the authority of a manager who'll keep track of the process in
   case he or she is called on to testify.

7. In collecting documentation, make sure to segregate attorney-client privileged documents.

8. If employees need to be interviewed, have your attorney do so, preferably an outside counsel. It's important these interviews be conducted by an attorney, so they can remain privileged. And it's best to have them done by an outside attorney so that your in-house counsel isn't compromised in some way.

> **KEY TERM** **Discoverable** In the American legal system, *discovery* is the pre-trial phase in a legal action in which each party can obtain evidence from the opposing party. This is most often done through *interrogatories*, the production of documents, admissions, and depositions. If one party refuses to provide "discoverable" evidence the opposing party can seek a subpoena from the court.

Trial by Media—An Attorney's Worst Nightmare

What I've listed above are recommendations that your organization's attorney will probably put forward, and I believe as a crisis manager you should support them. They're helpful in protecting your organization legally.

At the same time, these steps won't solve all your organization's problems. Because there's a terrible truth to crises that attorneys often hate to acknowledge: You're not just dealing with the legal system. You're also dealing with public opinion, and your organization can be tried in the media and found guilty by the public long before it gets its day in court.

The reality is if the crisis you're facing is bad enough it *will* be covered by the news media. And to get through that gauntlet, you have to overcome what I've termed the "The Five Conundrums of Media Relations," as introduced back in Chapter 6.

1. A reporter has the right to challenge anything you say or write, but will bristle when you try to do the same to them.

2. A reporter can put words in a naive source's mouth via leading questions ("Would you say that ... ? Do you agree that ... ? Do you feel that ... ?") and then swear by the authenticity of those quotes.

3. The media will report every charge filed in a criminal or civil case despite the fact that a civil case, in particular, can make all sorts of

wild, unproven claims with coverage focusing far more on the allegations than on responses by a defendant.

4. The media usually carries a bigger stick than you through its ability to selectively report facts and characterize responses, and via the public perception that "if I saw it in/on the news, it must be true."

5. "Off the record" often isn't, and "no comment" means "I've done something wrong and don't want to talk about it."

The weakness of a crisis response that focuses solely on the legal aspects of any crisis is that it ignores the demonstrated reality that an organization can win its lawsuits and still end up losing in the court of public opinion. The organization may win all the lawsuits filed against it, but if it also loses its market share, or a significant part of it, or it sacrifices customer loyalty, what it's managed to do is win the battle and lose the war.

The outcome of a "trial by media" depends to an unfortunate extent on the quality of reporting, but if you're prepared to deliver your key messages, have been media trained, and can view the media as a gateway to important audiences (versus "the enemy"), you can optimize the results. Sometimes that means being quoted accurately. Sometimes that means a story that looks very good for "your side."

Attorney Marc Budoff, a partner at Budoff and Ross, whose practice emphasizes criminal defense, says that his worst "trial by media" experiences occur "when I am representing someone facing emotion-eliciting charges, such as vehicular manslaughter or breaching the public trust."

THE ATTORNEY IS NOT THE SPOKESPERSON

While I'm advocating close cooperation between attorneys and crisis managers, I'm not recommending you make your attorney your media spokesperson. At least, not unless they are uniquely talented and extremely well media trained. And even then you really need to think about it. No offense to our law school brethren, but when a crisis breaks the public doesn't want to hear from the company's or organization's attorney. We all know the attorney's job is mainly to prevent lawsuits, so having an attorney out front and center seems defensive, which is *not* what you want to appear during a crisis. So *vet* your public statements through your legal counsel, but don't put him or her in front of the cameras.

In those situations, he said, "The media tends to editorialize in the guise of reporting, pandering to the emotionalism of the public. There is no balance, and constitutional issues of due process and fair trial get pushed aside."

Educating the Jury Pool

In crisis situations where you're forced into a court trial, legal and crisis management can still work together. To give you an idea how, which of the following statements about a jury, civil or criminal, do you think are true?

- Prospective jury members never lie regarding their advance bias about a case.
- Jury members are always truly "peers" of the defendant.
- Jury members never talk about a case outside of jury deliberations, or read and watch TV about a case when sequestered, once directed not to do so by a judge.

If your answer is "none of the above," you begin to appreciate the potential value of crisis management for the purpose of educating a jury pool. Now, I'm aware, though not an attorney, that members of the bar are not allowed to influence a jury. And while it is unethical to attempt to influence prospective jurors, there is nothing unethical or unprofessional about having an accurate picture of your client presented to the media and other audiences.

> **KEY TERM** **Jury pool** The jury pool is essentially the general public, from which a jury is typically called and selected by the court system. The term does not reference the actual jury, but the broader range of the public from which the jury will be selected.

Any honest reporter (yes, there are honest reporters who might even acknowledge there are honest attorneys) will admit that he or she brings a natural bias and an institutional editorial perspective to a story. Journalists will do their best, in that context, to report in a "balanced manner," with the exception of columnists, who are often free to say pretty much what they please and not worry about "balance."

These media representatives are a gateway through which both plaintiff/prosecutor and defendant can communicate to potential jury members. It's the responsibility of counsel, with expert assistance as necessary, to direct media relations that can shift the balance of coverage.

What tactics can be used for this public education process? They include, but are not limited to:

- The use of spokespersons trained to deliver key messages to the media and other audiences.

- Educating employees of defendant or plaintiff's companies about what to say or not to say about the situation at hand when they're back home, out in the community that will eventually be the source of jurors.

- Advertorials—buying print space or broadcast time in which you can put content about your company, client organization designed to help balance misinformation that may already be in the public eye. This tactic is usually only employed if the media has consistently misreported the facts.

The battle for the hearts, minds, and votes of jury members does not begin in the courtroom. In my experience, advance communication begins immediately after a legal situation hits the media. It can work together with legal tactics to (a) preclude a case ever going to trial (assuming that's a desired outcome for either side of the issue) or (b) affect public perception sufficiently to enhance either side's chance of a favorable outcome in court.

Manager's Checklist for Chapter 10

☑ The legal vs. crisis management debate is based on differing goals. Both are important.

☑ There's common ground. It's your job to find it.

☑ Integrate legal and crisis management strategies.

☑ Support reasonable legal strategies. But remember only crisis management strategies can prevent "trial by media."

☑ In cases facing trial, crisis managers can assist Legal by helping to educate the jury pool.

Crisis Management and the Publicly Owned Company

Throughout this book I refer to "organizations" when discussing entities facing a crisis. That's because any type of organization—including both for-profit organizations (companies) and not-for-profit organizations—are subject to a crisis, and the strategy for managing one is similar in most cases.

But I'm also aware that many readers of this book may work for companies—specifically publicly owned companies—and there are some unique aspects of crisis management that apply to that type of organization.

The Communications Pros and Cons of Public Companies

From a communications perspective, there are both advantages and disadvantages to being (or working for) a public company. One advantage and disadvantage is the opportunity to earn more media coverage (whether you want it or not), whether it's from major newspapers and magazines, TV shows or networks, radio shows, business and finance-related websites, or bloggers who cover the business scene or your particular business niche. This is because the media know that when you're a public company your owners—the shareholders—can be anyone.

This potential for media coverage can give you an advantage in building your brand, but you must temper such efforts with an awareness of the increased responsibility of a public company to communicate appropriately, play by the rules, maintain corporate transparency, and meet regulatory requirements.

A public company's key stakeholders extend far beyond the media, market researchers, customers, business partners, and employees. Those are fine for a private company. But in a public company you must also contend with financial analysts, shareholders, shareholder interest groups, and governmental regulators. This adds an entirely new audience—actually more than one—to the stakeholder audiences you must communicate with during a crisis.

In addition, since a public company is open to ownership by anyone (through the purchase of shares), rather than a single individual proprietor or a list of partners, it can come under intense scrutiny and attacks from investors of any size. The appearance of oppositional individual investors or investor groups at annual shareholder meetings is a fairly common occurrence, and increasingly these individuals and groups know how to use the media and the Internet to advance their agenda.

Former employees, if disgruntled, can also use the company's concern for its public reputation as leverage against it. And if a group of employees get together, the impact can be exponentially greater.

And, of course, whether generated by the Securities and Exchange Commission, by another governmental agency, or by Congress, there are

---

SMART

MANAGING

CRISIS MANAGEMENT AWARENESS

Based on the size of a public company, it may have various staff members or teams involved in communications with various stakeholders. For instance, Investor Relations staff will communicate with shareholders, analysts, and regulators; Public Affairs with government officials; Marketing with customers; and Public Relations with the news media. You must not leave Crisis Management out of the mix. Even if you don't have a separate crisis management team—few companies do—your communications teams should have an awareness of the need for crisis management, and you should either be handling this in-house or you should be working with an outside crisis management consultant or firm to prepare you for the inevitable and help you get through it.

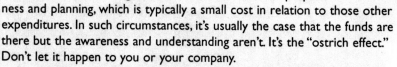

CRISIS PLANNING IS AN INVESTMENT

Be skeptical of claims by senior management that the company can't afford crisis preparedness or planning. If it has one or more people doing Investor Relations, Public Relations, Public Affairs, and/or Marketing, it has the funds to do crisis preparedness and planning, which is typically a small cost in relation to those other expenditures. In such circumstances, it's usually the case that the funds are there but the awareness and understanding aren't. It's the "ostrich effect." Don't let it happen to you or your company.

Instead, in putting forth the argument for crisis preparedness and planning, position it as it truly is—an investment. Public companies often spend millions to establish and promote their brand; the relatively small costs of crisis planning and training can pay huge dividends down the road when that brand is threatened.

disclosure regulations and legislation that put significant requirements on a public company to ensure transparency and fair dealing. The costs of noncompliance can be huge. Therefore public companies typically try hard to comply with them.

How a Public Company Should Respond to a Crisis

A public company should respond to a crisis the same way I outlined in Chapter 6 for any organization, but with a particular awareness that it has a different, wider audience than the typical organization. Here are some guidelines:

- Follow the Five Tenets as described: Be prompt, compassionate, honest, informative, and interactive.
- Develop tactics and messages aimed at all your audiences, those of the company's basic operations but also those related to public ownership—shareholders, investment groups, analysts, etc.
- Make sure these messages speak to the particular audience's concerns.
- Make sure you comply with regulatory requirements. It's best if you include either your CFO or your regulatory legal counsel in the crisis response team.
- Focus your media outreach efforts on business media. They are the ones most apt to convey your messages to business audiences.

■ Don't rely solely on the media to communicate with your key audiences such as shareholders, institutional investors, and analysts. Communicate with them directly through alternative and appropriate channels (your website, e-mails, phone calls, etc).

■ Avoid communications "silos." Investor relations, traditional PR, etc., should closely coordinate their activities to avoid inadvertently contradicting each other and putting the company in an embarrassing position.

How the Board Can Help ... or Hurt

With a privately owned company, the owner or partners are the face (and often the name) of the company. With a public company, however, this isn't always the case. Yes, there may be a Ford or a Heinz out there, but there is also a Cisco or a Google. A public company is owned by a number, if not a multitude, of shareholders. The board of directors is elected by said shareholders, and the board appoints the company's chief officers to carry out its day-to-day operations.

Regardless of ownership, in a crisis it's the responsibility of management, not the board, to protect the company. This isn't a problem as long as there's consensus on the board to allow the CEO (and his or her crisis response team) to do so. But that isn't always the case. Sometimes board members disagree with management's approach. It can get sticky.

I can't solve problems like that without being directly involved with the circumstances, but I can tell you what a board's position ought to be in a crisis situation:

■ The board needs to approve management's expenditures to manage the crisis.

■ The board needs to grant management the authority to manage the crisis.

■ The board needs to get out of the way.

Is this because board members don't know anything? Of course not. It's because in a crisis situation, time is of the essence. The time a company would normally take to make a decision isn't available in a crisis. As an example, some years ago I worked with a company that was facing an announcement by the federal government that could severely impact its operations. The CEO had assembled an excellent team to manage any downside from the announcement, including excellent messaging for the media and all stakeholder audiences. But a couple of board members had problems with the company's position, messaging, and strategy. Many board discussions ensued, and, since it was difficult to get all board members together for conference calls, weeks went by while meetings were arranged and directors argued various relatively minor points or wordsmithed a news release. As a result, when the crisis broke, there was nothing approved that could be used. There was no organized, effective counterargument to make. Instead there was a lot of wringing of hands over the bad publicity, which could have been avoided if the board had "gotten out of the way" and allowed management to do its job.

Does that mean board members can't help in a crisis? Not at all. Board members are often members of, or have significant contacts with, major shareholders or investor groups. These connections can be invaluable to you in communicating with shareholders *if* the board members stick to the script so the company can communicate with one voice. Here are a few tips on how a crisis manager can take advantage of the board in a crisis:

- Don't communicate with board members directly. Go through your CEO. Given his or her position, he or she will have much more credibility with the board than you do.
- Use your board members like you'd use your staff. Give them assignments—Okay, *ask* them to take on assignments. The point is you want to communicate with valuable audiences here, and you want to do it with the spokesperson with the most credibility to that audience.
- Make sure any messages you ask the board to communicate align with your key messages for other, less selective, audiences. It all has to hang together.
- If there's conflict on your board, or members who you don't trust to convey the company's messages, don't involve them in the process.
- Ask the board to stay out of the way. Better yet, have the CEO do that. The last thing you need, while the company is trying to communicate with one voice, is to have an errant board member talking to the

media. Rather, ask for a commitment by the board members that they won't talk to the media, that they'll let management handle that assignment.

Finally, make sure your board knows that you understand they have a fiduciary responsibility to the company. And your door is always open if they have questions or concerns. Better yet, have the CEO convey this message. If you're asking the board to trust you to manage the crisis, you owe it to them, as representatives of the stockholders, to answer their questions and take their concerns seriously.

> **SMART MANAGING**
>
> ### Act As If It's All Recorded
>
> The Internet continues to make it easier to read about, hear, and view skeletons in your closet. Corollary lesson: Conduct your business as if everything you write, say, and do might be recorded, and you'll avoid a lot of crises.

The Danger of Ignoring Threats

Let's take a look at a real-life crisis for a public company. I think this could help you realize what's at stake, and what strategies can (or should be) followed in a crisis situation.

The names have been changed to protect the . . . ostriches.

Stodgy Savings was a 50-year-old financial institution traded on the New York Stock Exchange. It had never had a significant crisis and had survived the Resolution Trust Corporation's purge of the U.S. savings & loan industry. Its stock was usually perceived as a solid, conservative "buy" based on consistent and predictable earnings. Its only internal public relations professional was focused on product promotion and investor relations were handled strictly by the CFO and CEO.

On a Monday afternoon, Stodgy's stock, then listed at $80 per share, begins to slip significantly, and by end of day was down to $70. There had been no company news to explain the slip and competitors' stock was doing well. After the market closed that day, when Stodgy's CFO was asked for a comment by a *Wall Street Journal* reporter, his response was, "We don't comment on stock price fluctuations."

On Tuesday, the slip continued, with the stock down to $65 and concerned analysts and investors swamping Stodgy's phone lines. The CFO and others stuck to their "no comment" position. Internally, they debated saying more but felt that their reputation and history would be sufficient to restore investor confidence.

On Wednesday afternoon, with the stock down to $55, a crisis management consultant was called in. He quickly determined that:

- The company had no idea why the sell-off started, nor had they made any attempt to find out why.
- There was, in fact, absolutely no business-based reason for lack of investor confidence.

The crisis manager suggested that Stodgy's CFO and CEO ask analysts following the company—the ones they had been essentially ignoring—what was "the word on The Street." The crisis manager concurrently made his own confidential inquiries with Wall Street sources. Both investigations revealed that:

- A rumor started, on Monday, that a prominent analyst had recommended "sell" on Stodgy's stock.
- Concurrently, for reasons having *nothing* to do with lack of confidence or any rumor, one institution sold off a large block of Stodgy stock.
- Other leading investors and investment advisors, monitoring the usual sources of Wall Street facts and rumors (Note: This situation occurred before the Internet was much of a factor in communications; today, rumor-spreading would have been far worse), saw the large block sell-off, heard the "sell" rumor, and assumed that they were related. The absence of communication by Stodgy acted to confirm their suspicions. The sell-off started in earnest.
- The analyst who allegedly had recommended "sell" claimed he hadn't done so, although there was hearsay that he'd made such a recommendation verbally, albeit not in a formal report.
- Perception had, indeed, become reality.

By then it was late Thursday afternoon. The stock was down to $45. Company management finally agreed to start presenting information to assuage the fears of investors. Overnight, a fact sheet highlighting the company's fiscal and management strengths was created and used by company executives to start calling analysts, major investors, and media who followed the stock. Plans for future written communication and investment community meetings were initiated.

By Friday, the stock leveled out at $40 and climbed back up to $50 by the end of the following week, but too much damage had been done. The stock never recovered to its previous levels during the subsequent two years, after which Stodgy was acquired by a larger firm, for a value well below what it would have sold for earlier.

During the weeks after the sell-off, investors and analysts told company representatives, "Why didn't you call back? Why didn't you comment? When you didn't say anything, we were sure something was wrong!" There were hundreds of expressions of disappointment and betrayal, of trust broken, irrevocably.

The bottom line: It's reasonable and probably legally prudent to have a policy of not commenting on minor stock price fluctuations, but to have no flexibility in a communications policy invites disaster. And to underestimate the power of rumors virtually *guarantees* disaster.

FOR EXAMPLE

POTENTIAL CRISES FOR PUBLIC COMPANIES

There are many potential crises for privately owned companies. For a publicly own company, the list is even longer. Given that crises can come in so many ways with so many variables, it's impossible for me to give you a step-by-step outline on how to handle every possible crisis.

Generally, you will be well served to follow the guidance provided in this book for the majority of crises. But for a public company there are unique challenges you may want to engage a specialist in dealing with. These include (among many others):

- A hostile takeover attempt by another company
- A sudden, steep decline in your share price
- Significant shareholder opposition at your annual shareholders' meeting
- A charge by a governmental agency that you have violated a disclosure law or regulation
- A consumer boycott of your products for whatever reason
- A finding by governmental or even nongovernmental scientists that your product may be dangerous to the public
- A product recall triggered by your own internal quality control program

Mergers and Acquisitions

Mergers and acquisitions (a.k.a. business combinations) often create a crisis or near-crisis situation for public companies that engage in them. Why? Because any time you take two entities accustomed to operating independently and try to combine them, there are challenges.

But they also offer a great opportunity to demonstrate to senior management why crisis-related efforts are of such value to an organization. Here are some of the challenges raised by a business combination:

- Each company brings its own agenda to the table.
- Each company has its own, unique culture. Blending them can be a challenge.
- Senior management of either firm, who may feel threatened by the combination, can jockey for position.

Things move swiftly. There's little time to plan and proceed. Quite often business combination plans are kept secret until the last minute. This on its own presents a unique set of challenges.

How do you manage a business combination? Here are some guidelines:

1. Establish a specific schedule of what will happen and when.
2. Determine a point person to lead the charge. Generally this needs to be the PR chief for the company doing the acquisition.
3. Whoever is leading the communication effort (and his or her team) should coordinate with the PR chief and team of the company being acquired. Why? Because that company may have stakeholders the acquiring company doesn't have connections with but will want to communicate with to maintain their support.
4. It's vital to develop credible and consistent messaging. This messaging should not be based on the interests of either of the two companies; it should be based on the benefits to the customer.
5. All spokespeople for the combination must be on the same page. This means that the communications teams from both sides must participate in the process. Not always easy to make happen due to the time constraints of many combinations. But more than worth the effort.

GREAT FOR STAKEHOLDERS

I can't stress enough that when one company merges with or acquires another, the messages put out should not be why the combination is so great for the companies involved; they should be about why it's great for stakeholders.

Yes, you may be required by management to issue a news release about how this corporate officer is "pleased" or that one is "very pleased" by the combination, but if you know anything about the media you know those are the comments immediately edited out of a news release before it's used.

If you are forced to issue such a dead-on-arrival release, don't despair. You can use media interviews to convey the important messages about the combination to your stakeholders.

Just make sure you have all your messaging ready in advance, and all your spokespeople suitably rehearsed.

6. When possible, include spokespeople from both companies in the same interview. As long as they don't conflict in their statements (heaven forbid), this sends a consoling message that both parties are getting along and the combination will work out to benefit all.

On the Positive Side

A crisis is not always a "bad news" situation. Often it can carry—at least for one side—a lot of good news. Here's a hypothetical, but based on a real life situation.

The Midas Bank Story

Midas Bank, a multi-billion-dollar, publicly held institution based in the Midwest, was among several organizations vying to acquire Struggling Savings & Loan, a privately held, California-based bank. Although Struggling's balance sheet was a little lopsided, it had an 80-branch operation, all in California, with excellent customer and community relations. Midas, which already had 20 branches in California and hundreds elsewhere, was informed by Struggling's board that they were the first choice to acquire Struggling—and the powers-that-be had decided the deal would go through in two weeks. Only then were both in-house and external public relations personnel notified of the pending merger. It was agreed that Midas would take the lead in creating and originating day-of-acquisition announcements.

The deal was going to result, operationally, in more resources for Struggling's growth and improvement and improved service to customers, with no immediate branch closures or layoffs, with any duplication of services to be phased out by natural attrition. It would also result in a promising new profit center for Midas.

How It Was Managed

A crisis communications team was rapidly created to prepare for day-of-acquisition announcements and reaction. The team consisted of top management and legal representatives from both firms, Midas' director of corporate communications, and the crisis communications group of a PR firm based in California. Discussion was held, and agreement reached on:

- **Objectives:** Primary: Prevent customer panic and possible "run" on assets. Secondary: Impress Wall Street with wisdom of the deal, increasing value of Midas' stock.
- **Target Audiences (internal and external):** including Midas/Struggling employees, Midas/Struggling customers, Midas/Struggling key community contacts, Midas/Struggling major vendors, Midas' investors and Wall Street contacts. Plus media serving all of the above. *Employees* were perceived as *the* most important audience because, for better or worse, employees were the "frontline" PR people for both companies. If they were happy with the deal, they would pass that sense of confidence on to others.
- **Key Messages:** Three "most important for all audiences" messages about business transaction, plus one to three additional key messages, as needed, specific to individual audiences. For example, a key message for employees was "you're keeping your job, and with improved benefits."
- **Day of Announcement PR Activities:** Letters from CEOs of both firms to every member of every target audience, delivered by the most expeditious method (varied from audience to audience). News releases and other news materials customized for different types of media (business, consumer, financial, trade). Spokespersons made available for interviews (after pre-announcement training). Instructions for branch personnel on how to answer inquiries and handle any media that

showed up on their doorstep. Teleconference between Midas/Struggling management and Wall Street contacts, including media, while Midas' CEO, CFO, and other Investor Relations team members made time to answer calls from the investment community.

The situation on which this case history is based occurred before the Internet became a PR tool. If it happened today, there would also have been a "virtual newsroom" created online for media use as well as a special page for customers, both of which would have been updated instantly as needed.

- **Post-Announcement PR Activities:** Ensuring that all important non-media audiences hear of any changes resulting from the merger directly from the company before they were mentioned in the press. Proactively monitoring media interest and providing in-depth briefings to longer-lead journalists. Implementing community relations activities to introduce "the Midas touch" to communities where they would now have branches. Conducting research to ensure that important messages have been received and believed by all target audiences.

Manager's Checklist for Chapter 11

☑ When it comes to a crisis, there are both positive and negative aspects of being a public company.

☑ There are many restrictions to communications when you're a public company. Make sure you know them.

☑ When responding to a crisis, understand the underlying rules are the same, but the audiences may be much larger and more extensive.

☑ Your board can help you in a crisis, or hurt you.

☑ Monitor changes in your value, and when they are extreme, find out why and deal with them.

☑ Combinations with other businesses can be your greatest test, but they can also be a great example of crisis management.

Chapter 12

Cultural Issues in Crisis Management

When I launched my Crisis Manager online newsletter in February 2000, at the start of the new century, I started with a few dozen readers—mostly business contacts and friends—all of whom were located in the United States. Today we have thousands of readers in 75 countries and have become required reading for management at a number of prominent companies. I don't mention this to tout my own success (I don't make any money from my eZine), but to point out that the awareness of the need and value of crisis management has grown exponentially in the past decade or so, and it's done so on a worldwide basis.

Why? I suspect for a simple reason: the globalization of both business and communications. As companies and organizations have grown globally, their vulnerabilities

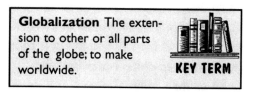

Globalization The extension to other or all parts of the globe; to make worldwide. **KEY TERM**

to crises and their need to manage them have increased as well, and as has been discussed in previous chapters, the Internet has exacerbated every crisis, and even been the primary focus for many of them.

Globalization, or the breakdown of national barriers to economic activity, is a fact, and it needs to be taken into account in crisis manage-

---

FOR EXAMPLE

ALL OVER THE WORLD

Globalization may seem like one of those abstract buzzwords you hear from talking heads on TV, but consider:

- It's highly unlikely that any of the clothes you're wearing were made in the USA.
- Many of the fruits and vegetables at your supermarket were grown in other countries (especially when it's winter in North America).
- The microchips used in your computer were probably manufactured in Asia.
- The page you're reading these words on may very well be made of paper produced from timber from Brazil.

The point is that globalization is all around us in our daily lives, and it doesn't look like it's going away. But does it impact our crisis management efforts? The short answer in many cases is—yes.

---

ment. Many companies now operate on a multinational level (even an American company with American owners or primarily American shareholders). Their raw materials may come from other countries, or be processed in other countries, and their products even manufactured in other countries before being delivered to the United States for distribution and sale. Or they're an American company with branches overseas. Or they're a service-oriented company and many of their employees are based abroad.

And companies aren't the only organizations dealing with globalization. If you work for a nonprofit, or an NGO (nongovernmental agency), chances are your operations involve more than Americans and American audiences.

It's an issue that involves most of us.

On top of that, there's another social dynamic impacting organizations—immigration. While business partners and supply chains of all types change internationally, the demographic dynamics at home are changing, too. It would be nice if in our communications we could assume all our stakeholders speak English—sorry, not always. Based on where you are in the United States, and of course on the situation, you need to consider whether your crisis communications need to be in both English and Spanish, and whether you need to include Hispanic media in your outreach. If you want to reach all your audiences you might need to.

The Reason? Your Stakeholders

If you work for a company where your entire operation—materials, processing, manufacturing, distribution, sales and service—happens within the United States, you may not need to worry so much about cultural issues. But if you're one of the other 99 percent of us, you do.

Why? Because crisis management is all about mitigating the damage a crisis may cause to an organization, and that's directly related to the organization's stakeholders since *they* are the ones in a position to most damage the organization.

If your stakeholders are limited geographically, you may not need to concern yourself with cultural issues. But most companies and organizations aren't in that position anymore. As I've mentioned, most are today operating multinationally, which means they may have stakeholders anywhere in the world. And that means they have stakeholder audiences with potentially entirely different expectations of how the organization will deal with a crisis.

A crisis can bring into sharp relief the cultural differences in your stakeholder audiences that are normally invisible during day-to-day operations. To be effective, your crisis communications must be sensitive to these varying cultural values.

And, if your organization has a crisis that occurs overseas, the challenge grows. Differences in time zones, languages, local laws, varying levels of support available from local authorities—all of these variables and many others can raise significant barriers to effective crisis management.

CROSS BORDER CHALLENGES

I recently worked with an international trade association facing a crisis. Most of its members were American companies, but not all of them. Several of the board members were located overseas—South America, China, etc. And most of the companies had their processing facilities in other countries. With all the time zones involved, just putting a teleconference together was a challenge. Imagine how much more difficult it was to develop strategies and messaging that addressed the audiences in all those different cultures.

DON'T ASSUME ANYTHING

When dealing with a crisis in a multicultural context, don't assume you understand anything. No, I didn't say "everything," I said "anything."

Of course there are some commonalities that extend across all cultures—we all love music; we all mourn when someone dies—but you'd be surprised how easy it is to misunderstand how another culture will interpret something you think is completely obvious.

For example, in many cultures an apology has an entirely different meaning than it does to Americans. We assume when you offer an apology you're accepting responsibility for whatever bad thing happened. Not so in some other cultures, where, instead, an apology is seen as an expression of sympathy without any acceptance of blame at all.

Another example is the prospect of litigation. A lot of crisis messaging in America is built around the need to avoid litigation. In many other cultures, either because they don't have the same sort of legal system we do or they simply have different values, the threat of litigation over a crisis is much smaller.

Those are just two examples of disconnects between what you may think a foreign audience wants to hear in a crisis and what they really want to hear.

How to Manage a Crisis with Multicultural Stakeholders

Understand There Are Differences

The first step is simple. Don't be an "Ugly American." (For younger readers, that was a best-selling novel in 1958 about Americans going all over the world expecting everyone to cater to us.) If you have stakeholders in other countries, living in different cultures, don't assume they think like Americans do. Don't assume they have the same values, needs, expectations, or even modes of understanding. They may in some ways, but they may not in others.

Tap Your Local Talent

The best way and primary strategy in managing your crisis multiculturally is to include members of your team in those locations and cultures in your crisis response. No, they may not be members of your primary response team (who are probably huddled around a conference table at your home office). But you should discuss your strategies and messages with them to ensure they'll fly with your other cultural audiences, or can be adapted to do so.

Remember Language

Remember language, which is often a significant cultural barrier. You may need to (quickly) translate some of your communications for foreign audiences. Have people or resources that can do this for you arranged in advance, based on the various cultures where you organization operates or has stakeholders.

Don't Issue Contradictory Statements

At the same time, remember that since the Second World War, English has progressively become the *lingua franca* of the planet. Meaning that whatever you post in English on the Internet will probably be read and understood by an audience as diverse as a college kid in Bolivia or a high schooler in South Korea. Don't issue anything in English that doesn't align with what you're saying on the ground in India, or Argentina, or Kenya.

Remember Nonverbal Messages

It's not just about language. There are many other forms of communication besides verbal. For instance, in America it might be acceptable to parade a series of spokespeople before the cameras, but in many countries that could be seen as trying to hide something. They're not impressed by teams of spokespersons or lawyers speaking on behalf of the organization. They, even more than we do, expect *one* person to stand up and deal with the issue. (Maybe they're on to something.)

Tap Your Local Allies

When facing a crisis in a foreign country, you don't always have to play defense. It's assumed your presence or your stakeholders there are a benefit to the community. If that's true, when facing a crisis put a call out to your employees, business partners, and other supporters to voluntarily speak on your behalf. It may not manage the specific crisis, but a multitude of public voices on your side can definitely help your position and help protect your reputation.

Manager's Checklist for Chapter 12

☑ Both globalization and immigration have created new challenges for crisis management.

☑ Globalization especially creates whole new groups of stakeholders.

☑ When dealing with other cultures, don't assume they think like you do. It's not that they disagree, they may just have a different way of understanding.

☑ If you have team members or allies in other cultures, tap into their knowledge to help you.

☑ Adapting your tactics and messaging to another culture is a sign of respect and will help your crisis management efforts.

Chapter

13

Crisis Management Tools

I n many ways crisis management is an art, but there's also a lot of science that goes into doing it effectively. Science in the form of technology. Crisis management is a *communications* practice—we're not digging ditches or building houses here. But without the proper tools, you'll be as ineffective as a ditch digger without a shovel or a carpenter without a nail gun (nobody in the house-building business uses hammers anymore). So let's talk about the tools you'll need to do crisis management the way it needs to be done today.

Connectivity and Accessibility

If a crisis manager can't get online, retrieve files, and/or make phone calls when he or she needs to, effectiveness is severely impaired. Not to mention upsetting your boss or client. If there's anyone who needs to walk their talk on connectivity and accessibility, it's those of us who work in the field of crisis management. Anyone who might end up becoming engaged in crisis response needs to have a very high level of connectivity and accessibility, or at least be able to ramp up those levels as needed.

One caveat: My experiences come from running a small consultancy operating as a virtual agency. What works for me may have to be modified based on your situation. But I trust readers of this book will be able to identify where the differences lie and adapt for their own success.

Staying Online

I need Internet and e-mail access to operate at peak efficacy. Ideally, I want to be able to continuously use my Outlook-based e-mail system. Yet I've found, often the hard way, that:

- Some locations, even major hotels, still don't have currently function-ing Internet access.
- Sometimes my local ISP "goes down" for an indeterminate period.
- Client locations, given today's IT security needs, seldom afford me the ability to send e-mail out from Outlook, although I may be able to access Web-based e-mail if they will at least allow me to run my browser through their server.
- On the go—even from the back of a taxi—I might need to receive or send e-mail or access the Internet.

TRICKS OF THE TRADE

BE REDUNDANT

The key to maintaining connectivity and accessibility, i.e., staying online, is redundancy. Systems, alas, go down or are unavailable, often when we need them most—ISP service gets interrupted, you're outside the range of your smartphone service's nearest transmitter or you can't find a Wi-Fi location no matter how hard you look. Don't be that guy or gal who's out of contact when you're needed most. To manage a 21st-century crisis, you absolutely must have more than one system in place that provides you access to your e-mail and the Web.

How do I cope with these variable challenges? Here's how:

- I don't rely on a single connectivity service.
- I use my mobile hotspot (available from all major cellular carriers) when no broadband is available (or when I want more security than you can get on an open public Wi-Fi service). I have two computers, my desktop and my notebook (usually used for travel but fully capa-ble of replacing my desktop in a few minutes). At home or traveling, I can connect to the local broadband service by ethernet cable or wire-lessly. I use my smartphone when necessary. Face it, typing on a com-puter (at least for an experienced keyboard user) is one heck of a lot easier than thumbing a smartphone keyboard. However, I have found

<table>
<tr><td>

HAVE MULTIPE ACCESS

Go to the copyright page of this book and see when it was published. If it was more than a few years ago, don't depend entirely on my advice here. Communications technology is changing fast. For all I know in a couple of years someone will invent a device that provides all the backup systems I talk about here in one product. All you'll need to do is buy it, read the owner's manual, and do a bit of programming. But we don't have that device today, so a word to the wise: Have multiple access systems for e-mail and the Web. It can mean the difference between being able to manage a crisis, and being overwhelmed by it.

CAUTION

</td></tr>
</table>

my smartphone to have multiple uses in the area of connectivity and accessibility. First, it gives me a third Internet service to use if no others are available. Second, I can and do maintain a separate smartphone e-mail address for my clients to use in the event of urgent communications and in the event that my primary e-mail server is down. And, oh, yeah—it's a telephone, too, one that has powerful data duplication capability (i.e., storing every contact and appointment from my Outlook program). And if you haven't tried it on your smartphone, I find that the "dictate text" function on mine (currently a Droid2, formerly a Blackberry) is accurate—I use it all the time for text messaging and e-mail.

▪ I have two alternate e-mail addresses I can use if my primary e-mail server goes down—one on Google (gmail) and one on Yahoo!.

I even have a two-piece backup plan for the possibility of my electricity being out longer than my notebook computer battery can last: (1) a power cord for the notebook computer that allows it to be charged from my car's battery and (2) a cord that allows my mobile hotspot to be charged from the notebook computer. This could prove to be particularly important in the event some natural disaster interrupted power for an extended time. Of course, I also have to make sure I have gas in the car!

Okay, You're Online ... Now What?

Today the most vital tools for crisis preparedness and response are those that involve:

- Training, planning, and crisis team response, such as Webcasting services
- Monitoring services to see what's being said about your organization
- Coverage-tracking
- Web-response

Webcasting

We used to call this videoconferencing, but that's pretty much gone the way of the dodo since the Web has made accessibility easier and more affordable to wider audiences. Today, using services such as Skype, ooVoo, or WebEx, you can quickly bring in numbers of participants for a "virtual" meeting complete with live camera action using Webcams. These services can be helpful in training exercises, planning discussions, and especially crisis-team huddles, where they allow you to not only talk to your opposite numbers, but see them, as well.

Monitoring Service

Using one or more monitoring services is essential in crisis management. At a bare minimum, you should have Google Alerts set up for your organization's name or, if you're conducting a specific campaign of some kind, the campaign's name. Additionally you should be regularly tracking and analyzing mentions of your organization on other websites. Not just news coverage, but by manual use of search engines.

Sound like a lot of work? Not as much as you'd think, particularly if you take advantage of a useful tool offered by Google. If you add a Google Search Bar to your Web browser, it offers you two choices when you enter a search term: (a) Search Web—your regular Web search and (b) Search Site—it digs down into the site you're visiting at that time. So instead of having to go through all the pages of the site, you enter your organization in the Search Site window and it will give you a list of any pages on which that term is mentioned. It's not foolproof, it sometimes produces odd results, but it's generally accurate.

Additionally, you can use "all in one" tools such as TweetDeck or Hootsuite to simultaneously monitor what's being said about you on Twitter, Facebook, and LinkedIn, while also using the same tools to post messages to any of those social media sites.

Finally, if no one on your staff is Web savvy, contact any local college or university that has a public relations program and ask about getting an intern who understands how to use the tools I'm talking about in this chapter. Such part-time employees will work their you-know-whats off on your behalf for minimum wage because college credit is also involved, and because they're doing something they love to do.

Coverage-Tracking Services

There are lots of coverage-tracking services available. Some are available through media relations services such as CustomScoop, Vocus, Cision, or MyMediaInfo. Others, such as eWatch, are available through wire services like PRNewswire. In evaluating which service to use, consider the following:

- **Cost.** Some are priced much higher than others. They may or may not be worth it, depending on your needs.
- **Coverage.** Some include non-Internet coverage; some don't.
- **Analytics.** Most offer some evaluation of your coverage; but frankly some are better at drilling down to what's important to you than others are.

Web Response

Let's face it, many organizations—and especially most businesses—see the Internet as a marketing tool and nothing more, a way to sell more products and services, not as a way to have dialog with their stakeholders. Sure, they have a "customer service" tab on their home page, but you might as well be calling them on the phone.

And when a crisis breaks, they're often very skittish about mentioning it on their website. After all, the website is a sales tool, right? Let's not tell prospective customers we may have a problem.

Enter the need for Web-response services, services that let you create a new website quickly—I mean within minutes—to address the crisis at hand. To provide information, offer support for victims, communicate your key messages, and many other purposes.

There are a number of services that do this. Two with which I'm familiar are MissionMode and Pier Systems. They both provide a fully integrated Internet platform for internal and external crisis management. For example, communication team members log in to the system from wherever they are located and from the private site can develop materials, collaboratively edit, and upload digital files and track draft changes. Designated approvers can approve materials online and, once approved, information is instantly uploaded to the external public site and e-mailed or faxed from within the system to any number of databases of stakeholders managed in the system. Inquiries coming in from the public site are tracked and managed and new sites related to specific incidences or issues can be launched within seconds by the designated users.

The advantages of having these communication functions on an Internet platform are considerable. Equally important is the fact that Pier and MissionMode are hosted services, which means companies and organizations don't need to significantly expand their Internet hosting services to accommodate the traffic they could experience in a major crisis.

As to Social Media ...

This is being written in early 2011. Why is that related to the topic?

Because if you're reading this any later than six months post-publication, chances are a good part of the information is outdated. The Internet is the embodiment of rapid change and innovation, and even a self-admitted geek like your author has a hard time keeping up with all the communications tools available, only some of which are clearly useful for crisis management.

The potential roles online tools end up playing aren't always obvious at first. Twitter started strictly as a social networking tool. But then people were using Twitter to communicate from the site of natural disasters. Soon, others were "tweeting" breaking news of all sorts, while some Twitter users found it was a great way to instantly complain about ... anything. Twitter has evolved, as of this writing, into a way for those who intend your organization harm to start immediately blasting your reputation.

Here are some tools I use to manage crises today (like I said, I take no responsibility for their obsolescence by the time you read this):

- **Pipl and Zabasearch**—Surprisingly useful search engines for information about individuals. Some of the info is free, some is (usually low) fee-paid. I can pretty much guarantee you that this is where private investigators start looking for missing people without having to call in a favor at the local police department.

- **TweetBeep**—The Twitter equivalent of Google Alerts.
- **Topsy**—Twitter's own search tool. It allows you to search by location, keywords you want to include, and even sentiment on particular tweets.
- **TweetTag**—Search what's been on Twitter over the past 24 hours.
- **Twoogle**—This is a new service that lets you search Google and Twitter at the same time.
- **WhosTalkin.com**—A social media search engine that tracks a wide range of blogs, major news portals, social networking sites, even images and forums.

You don't have to be a geek to take advantage of these tools, but you do need to employ one who has sufficient training and experience to collect accurate information about how your most important asset—your reputation—is being managed online. Technophobes have no place as corporate leaders in the 21st century.

Again, by the time you read this there may be a whole host of new programs or applications available to monitor and communicate through social media. Just do a Google search for "best social media tools." The point is to use the tools at hand to monitor and influence those things being said about your organization as they occur ... whatever they happen to be today.

The In-Person Approach—A Tool Not to Be Forgotten

Many of the tools I've talked about in this chapter are intended to help you and your crisis response team manage a crisis through electronic media—e-mail, websites, etc. That's because today so many organizations have stakeholders, including the media and the public, who are impossible to reach any other way. So it makes sense to use the tools that allow you to reach them.

But if there's a stakeholder audience you can communicate to through alternative methods, consider doing so. Especially your internal audiences.

During the recent economic downturn, one of my clients had to carry out several RIFs (reductions in force, a corporate term for lay-offs). In fact over a three-year period they had to conduct five of these RIFs, cutting their staffing by as much as 90 percent to stay afloat. Every time, the CEO not only put out an e-mail to all employees explaining the RIF, he also visited up to 15 locations each time to meet with employees personally, hear their concerns, and outline what the company would be doing to maintain their benefits and help them find other work.

These exchanges were difficult for both sides, but the result was nobody called the media to complain, and nobody filed a lawsuit claiming wrongful termination. The employees affected by the crisis appreciated that the CEO came to meet with them face-to-face, and though they didn't like the company's decision, they appreciated being treated with respect as demonstrated by the CEO showing up and taking responsibility for the decision.

This sort of approach isn't always possible; in fact, today it's increasingly less possible. Most organizations have stakeholder audiences in far-flung areas, as well as audiences ready to comment or respond in a "New York minute" or less with messages that can go viral in minutes.

Still, when it can be applied, the personal, in-person approach is a crisis management tool you ought not to leave out of your toolkit. It can not only be highly effective, sometimes it's just the right thing to do.

Emergency Preparedness Checklist for Small Businesses

Here's an outstanding tool to use in your crisis management efforts. It's a checklist for small businesses put together by the American Red Cross and FedEx. I include it here, shamelessly, because it just might save somebody's life.

Developing an emergency preparedness plan is one of the most important strategic decisions you will make as a small business owner. Consider how a natural, human-caused or public health disaster could affect your employees, customers, and workplace. Would business operations continue? Preparing your small business doesn't have to be time consuming or expensive. Ask yourself the four questions below and use this checklist to help you prepare your business to stay in business.

1. **How vulnerable would your business be if a disaster or other emergency were to occur?**

Know your region and the types of disaster most likely to have an impact on your business.

- Find out what emergencies have occurred in the past and what impact these had on other businesses in your area.
- Consider your facility's physical capacity to resist damage and proximity to flood plains, seismic faults, dams, hazardous materials, nuclear power plants, and other hazards.
- Consult with your insurance agent and learn what coverage is available and what precautions to take for disasters that may impact your business. Remember, many general policies do not cover earthquake and flood damage.

Assess the capacity of your employees to prepare for and respond to an emergency.

- Are 10–15 percent of your employees trained in basic first aid and CPR techniques?
- Do all employees know how to identify individuals who are trained?
- Are employee roles clearly defined in the event of a disaster or emergency?
- Identify external emergency response resources that will provide assistance during a disaster or other emergency.

2. **Whom will you contact in an emergency, and what will they be able to provide?**

- Local and state police
- Fire department and emergency medical services organizations
- Local governmental officials, emergency management office
- Local American Red Cross chapter
- National Weather Service
- Telephone, water, gas, and electric companies
- Neighboring businesses

3. **What is your plan to protect the business and its employees before, during, and after an emergency?**

- Identify a First Aid team.
- Approximately 10–15 percent of your workforce should be trained in first aid and CPR so they can assist in times of disaster or emergency until help arrives.

Obtain necessary safety equipment.

- Budget for and purchase any safety equipment, first-aid kits, Automatic External Defibrillators (AEDs), fire extinguishers, smoke detectors, and shelter-in-place supplies that may be needed. Make sure employees know how to use and access these supplies.

Write a plan for responding to emergencies. Your plan should include:

- A system for warning employees about emergencies and communicating with employees and local emergency management officials during a disaster or emergency
- Considerations for the special needs of employees with disabilities and medical conditions
- Evacuation routes from your facility and an established location where employees should gather
- Provisions and a location for employees to shelter-in-place

Develop a Continuity of Operations Plan (COOP). This plan will help keep your business operating as it responds and recovers from the effects of a disaster or emergency situation. Here's how to start developing a COOP:

- Establish procedures for COOP activation.
- Identify essential business functions and staff to carry out these functions.
- Establish procedures with suppliers, vendors, and other businesses critical to daily operations.
- Create a plan for conducting business if the facility is not accessible and set up electronic backup systems for vital business files.
- Identify records and documents that must be readily accessible to perform essential functions and decide where these can be stored safely and retrieved quickly.

4. **What can we do to integrate emergency preparedness procedures into our everyday business operations?**

Educate employees. Consider partnering with community organizations to create comprehensive preparedness training. All employees should know:

- Their role during a disaster and the roles and responsibilities of key personnel at your facility
- Warning and communication procedures
- Evacuation and shelter-in-place procedures

Practice your plan

- Conduct regular evacuation, COOP activation, and shelter-in-place drills.
- Use the drills to assess the readiness of your employees and your facility.
- Involve both personnel and community responders in the evaluation process and use lessons learned to improve procedures and increase training as needed.

Encourage personal preparedness among employees. Your employees will be better able to help your business respond and recover from an emergency if they know how to prepare their homes and families.

- Offer first aid, CPR, AED, and preparedness training.
- Encourage your employees and their families to Get a Kit, Make a Plan, Be Informed. A free online education module is available to help them at *redcross.org/BeRedCrossReady.*
- Encourage employees to identify alternative routes for going to and from your facility.
- Remind employees to always keep their emergency contact information current.
- Help your community get prepared. Work with local community groups and governmental officials to ensure that your community is prepared for disasters and other emergencies.
- Host blood drives.
- Work with your local Red Cross chapter to train community disaster education volunteers to conduct preparedness presentations.
- Contribute supplies and/or services to emergency efforts.
- Adopt a local school or school district and support their emergency preparedness programs.

Manager's Checklist for Chapter 13

☑ Staying connected and accessible is Rule #1 in crisis management.

☑ Redundancy is the key to staying online.

☑ The tools crisis managers need or can use are changing constantly—you must keep up.

☑ Stay abreast of social media tools and developments.

☑ Don't forget the human face of communication.

☑ Use the Emergency Preparedness Checklist.

Crisis Management Consultants

Only you and your organization can decide if you need an outside consultant to assist you with crisis prevention and the preparedness disciplines of planning, training, response, and messaging. I'm not here to tell you that you need such help. I *am* here, however, to help you navigate that process and maximize any investment you do decide to make in crisis management.

Since I started in this business almost 30 years ago, technology has caused the reach of media to become greater and greater. This explosion of media coverage—first through 24-hour cable TV news coverage and then through the Internet—has greatly extended the exposure of companies and organizations to crises of all kinds. Meaning today there is more chance of damage, and more need for crisis management.

Not surprisingly, the number of firms claiming to offer assistance in these areas has grown tremendously. In fact, today most PR firms and even some marketing companies claim they provide crisis management consulting and all manner of related services. Even some law firms are claiming to do so.

I can't talk about whether any firm other than my own can provide the level of expertise and service you'd need in a crisis situation. What I *can* talk about, though, is that managing a crisis isn't as easy as most PR firms make it sound. Crisis messaging is not PR messaging. Crisis media relations is not traditional media relations. Online reputation management is not the same as building your brand identity on the Web. Many of the technical tools may be the same, but the goals and the strategies differ considerably.

If your organization can't afford to hire an outside crisis management consultant, that's fine. That's what this book is for. Hopefully I'll give you enough information and guidance that you can handle a crisis on your own. But if you need to hire an outside consultant, either for crisis management in its entirety or for any one of its subsets, there are things you should know about hiring, contracting with, and working with an outside consultant.

How Do Crisis Management Consultants Operate?

Today, crisis management consultants typically work within one of three business models:

1. One or more individuals specialize in crisis management within the structure of a larger firm that primarily focuses on something else, e.g., public relations, marketing, or the legal profession.
2. A larger "brick and mortar" company wholly devoted to crisis management, which will often have a number of specialists all working for the same company (in the same building, hence the reference to building materials).
3. An independent consultant who runs what I call a "virtual consultancy," with a range of associated specialists he or she can call on depending on the needs of the client, and who work together using technology.

Regardless of their particular business model, a crisis management consultant operates in the same way that a legal or financial consultant does. An outside attorney, after all, is a consultant. So is an outside CPA or auditor. Meaning, they generally investigate an organizational situation and provide expert guidance on how to address it. They don't have authority and they don't call the shots—management does—but they are there to consult with management and help them call the shots correctly.

A CONSULTANT IS NOT A SPOKESPERSON

If you bring in an outside crisis management consultant to help you deal with a crisis, don't expect to make them the company's or organization's spokesperson. This is rarely, if ever, a good idea. Not that you should hide the fact you've hired a crisis manager. You shouldn't announce it to the general public, but it might be news your key stakeholders would welcome, since it's in their interest for you to survive the crisis. But the appropriate place for a consultant is in the background, out of the public eye, consulting.

In a crisis, your stakeholders and the public want to hear from the organization, from your CEO or someone else in authority, not a "hired gun." Don't make the mistake of putting your consultant in front of the cameras, or have them take interviews instead of your organization's spokesperson. Yes, it might be easier, but it's a bad idea.

Hiring a Crisis Management Consultant

There are two secrets to hiring the right crisis management consultant for your organization.

First, look for someone who has experience in your area, whether you're a company, a not-for-profit, a governmental agency, or something else. There are so many unique aspects to crises in different fields that it's smart to get someone to help you who has already worked in your field.

Second, hire them now. Don't wait for a crisis to break. For years my website has said: "If you have a breaking crisis NOW, call _____." And I can't tell you how often that's exactly the way I get new clients. I wish it weren't. I wish they'd have called me a year ago, or even six months ago. I might have been able to help them prepare—and saved them a lot of money in lost revenues, legal expenses, or shareholder value.

You may be thinking, "I don't want to hire a crisis management consultant now. We're not having a crisis. It's not in the budget." No, it's probably not. But it's possible to set up a relationship with a crisis management consultant before a crisis hits, and to have them talk with you about what you need, how to implement it, and how it can be affordable. The bad idea is to call a consultant and ask them to drop everything to handle your particular crisis *now*. Be proactive. It will save you money in the long run.

CONSULTANT AS MEDIA TRAINER

Don't hire a crisis management consultant who can't provide you with media training. Yes, I say elsewhere in the book that the media isn't the only way to communicate to your stakeholders in a crisis, but the reality these days is that you have to be equipped to deal with the media to manage a crisis. Make sure your crisis management consultant is an experienced media trainer, and has worked in the media, especially as a journalist, themselves. Ideally they, too, are regularly interviewed by the media and you can watch their interviews—so you know they practice what they preach.

How do you find a crisis management consultant? There's no trade association for crisis managers you can go to for recommendations. And the last thing you want to do is look in your phone book. There's no Crisis Management listing. More importantly, with the technology we have today you no longer have to look for somebody in your city or even state. At any given time my colleagues and I are working with clients all over the United States and even overseas.

Instead, try doing an online search for "crisis management." Add in any keywords that apply to your industry. You'll probably find in the first few pages a number of consultants you can consider.

Once you've found a list of consultants to consider, how do you know who's the best choice? Here is a list of questions to ask any potential crisis consultant. The answers should provide you with insights critical to making an informed decision about using his or her services.

1. What's your background in crisis management? How long have you practiced, and in what capacities?

2. Can you give us some examples of your work in this field? Please be specific.

3. Have you ever worked in our industry or area of operations?

4. Do you have a crisis plan you personally prepared that we can review? Was this plan used? What was the result?

5. Does your training include how to communicate with both media and nonmedia audiences?

6. How will you teach us how to maintain the skills we have learned from you? Please be specific.

7. Can you show us anything you've written about this topic and/or articles in which you've been interviewed?

8. If the stuff hits the fan, can you also provide us with spot advice on what we should do or say?

If you want your consultant to also offer media training, ask questions like these:

1. Have you worked as a journalist yourself?

2. If yes, what type of journalist were you (e.g., anchor, investigative reporter)?

3. If no, what is the basis for your understanding of the media?

4. Does your training prepare us both for routine interviews and for crisis-level interviews?

5. How long have you been a media trainer?

6. Can you show us anything you've written about this topic and/or articles in which you've been interviewed?

7. Can you show us any instances such as videos where you've been interviewed yourself?

Hiring a Web Consultant

Hopefully, once you've read this book, you'll feel that you can take on the challenge of facing a crisis for your organization yourself or with your staff. You may need some help in a few specialized areas, such as media training, but overall you're confident you can conduct the preparedness, planning, training, and message development for your organization that you need to do.

Then you think—but what about the Web?

Let's face it, the Internet is the world's biggest medium now (as I discuss in Chapter 9) and it also represents the biggest challenge—and opportunity—from a communications standpoint.

Crisis management on the Web isn't just about having a website, though obviously your website should be a major component of your online communications. If you're going to be successful managing your crisis on the Web, you have to know how to *use* the Internet beyond having a website. Meaning you'll be well served having an expert on your side who understands the technical side of the Web as well as its strategic possibilities.

Today, though, every Web designer on the planet seems to promise expert search engine optimization and a high ranking on search engines. And some actually know how to do this. But a lot don't. Here is a list of questions to ask any Web consultant whom you're considering for your crisis management team:

1. What's your background as a Web consultant?
2. What are the various projects you've worked on?
3. Does any of your background include working in crisis situations? What samples can you provide us?
4. Can you teach us how to maintain a high search engine ranking for whatever Web presence we implement?
5. What steps do we need to take to ensure a regular, highly ranked Web presence for our online communications?
6. Does your training include how to deal with nontraditional media, e.g., social media?
7. How will you teach us to maintain the skills we have learned from you? Please be specific.
8. Does your training prepare us to do Web communications ourselves, or will we have to work through you?
9. Can you show us anything you've written about this topic and/or articles in which you've been interviewed or quoted?
10. If the stuff hits the fan, can you also provide us with spot advice on what we should do?

If you're doing your crisis management yourself, find a Web consultant you're comfortable can provide the online expertise you need. You'll be glad you did.

And the good news is, if you bring in a qualified outside crisis management consultant, they'll already have access to accomplished Web consultants who know how to get things done right.

> **CAUTION**
>
> **CONSULTANT AND SEO**
> If a Web consultant promises you first-page search engine ranking, ask how they will accomplish it. The reality is today with so many people aware of the value of SEO, it's not easy to achieve such results. Unless your consultant can articulate a plan to make this happen, you may be dealing with someone who's selling the sizzle and not the steak. Buyer beware.

Contracting with a Crisis Management Consultant

As mentioned above, crisis management consultants work with organizations just like other outside consultants do, whether they're attorneys, accountants, auditors, or some other professional. There are, however, certain things you should be mindful of in contracting with an outside consultant.

It's important in contracting with any consultant to clearly define the Scope of Work in the agreement. What services *exactly* are they expected to perform? And this isn't the place to put in the usual company boilerplate for employees about "and any other duties ..." That won't fly with a consultant any more than it will fly with your attorney.

In addition to any agreed fees, reimbursables are typically passed along to the client organization at cost. Examples would be airfare, hotels, and meals when required to travel. It's not generally accepted for these to be marked up.

It's very likely you won't have to devise a service agreement with a crisis management consultant. If they're experienced in the field, they'll have a standard agreement to provide you. All you'll need to do is run it through your legal department.

When it comes to compensation, consultants charge differently. Some will charge a monthly retainer fee; some will charge an hourly rate. There's no right or wrong way here; I personally think an hourly rate is fairer to the client.

Don't be surprised if your crisis management consultant asks for an up-front payment against which services can be charged (with written assurance that unused funds will be refunded). If they do this they aren't being greedy; in fact it probably shows that they're experienced. Those of us who've worked in the business awhile know that not all crisis clients survive no matter what. And nobody wants to work for nothing.

In contracting with a consultant, make sure there's language in your agreement that clearly states that the agreement is confidential and proprietary, and that neither party will divulge any of the agreement without the agreement of both or pursuant to a court order. The reason is you will be sharing proprietary knowledge on both sides, so both sides should be protected.

Make sure the agreement has a reasonable cancellation clause. You don't want to be paying a consultant monthly fees a year after the crisis is over.

In the course of crisis management activities, a lot of what's called "work product" or "deliverables" can be created—vulnerability audits, plans, memos, messaging, etc. Make sure you are granted all right, title, and interest in such "work product." There can be other legalese involved, but I think you get the point. You don't want somebody taking the crisis plan you've worked on for two months and selling it to a competitor.

Your consultant might ask to be compensated for responding to a subpoena, deposition, or similar action. You should include that in the agreement. It's not only fair; it's also a good idea.

Working with a Consultant

Assuming you and your organization have decided not to go it alone, and instead to bring in a crisis management consultant, what can you expect?

It depends on where you are in the process. If you've brought someone in before a crisis has broken, you can expect them to fulfill their scope of work and to provide deliverables as agreed. Of course, it will make that more likely to happen, and ensure a better quality product, if you provide them with the access they need. I've seen too many circumstances where a company agrees to a vulnerability audit, but then key personnel aren't available to be interviewed. Or a crisis plan needs to be developed, but nobody's told IT they need to cooperate. Make sure your organization's commitment to the crisis preparedness process is endorsed at the top, and that endorsement is communicated to all parts of the organization. Half a crisis plan is worth about as much as no crisis plan.

But assuming your crisis is about to break or has already broken, you should expect your crisis management consultant to be on the job 24/7. This is one way that a crisis management consultant differs from your other consultants. You probably can't call your auditor at 11:30 on a Saturday night with a problem. With a professional crisis manager, you can. It comes with the territory. Crisis managers understand that crises can happen at any time; they therefore need to be available at any time. It's a big world, and companies and organizations have operations worldwide in any given time zone.

If your crisis management consultant says or performs as though he or she only works a 40-hour week, you may want to look for another one.

Outside of on-the-spot service, you also have the right to expect your crisis management consultant to become part of your team. And he or she should. Fact is, it's impossible for anyone—based on what you're asking them to do—to identify your organization's vulnerabilities, develop a plan to address potential

> ### GET AN EXPERT   SMART
>
> In working with a crisis management firm, handle it the same way you would any other consultant. A lot of   **MANAGING**
> consulting firms are great at sending out well-dressed, articulate reps to sell you on their service, then once they have it you're turned over to some junior staffer who hasn't nearly the talents or experience. Don't let this happen to you. It's true, the principal of the firm you're dealing with may not handle everything for you personally, but make sure they are turning it over to an expert at that activity and they are in the loop at all times.

threats, or get you to the point where you can respond, unless they are taken in as part of the organization. This is specifically why the standard crisis management agreement addresses the issue of confidentiality and propriety information.

You should also establish a structure for regular reporting with your consultant. This will, of course, have to be framed in the context of their scope of work, but regular, ongoing reporting of actions taken and objectives reached or not should be part of the process. This will help you do a number of things—gauge your progress, refine your strategies, and justify expenditures.

Of course in the midst of a crisis it may be difficult for you, your team, and your consultant to find the time to do much reporting, but that doesn't lessen its importance. Make the time to review at least where you are and what requires immediate attention. With modern technology a lot of reporting can be done in real time and, even if not, a few minutes on the phone can help greatly. If you don't pay attention to such things they can easily slip by and add to the crisis.

Manager's Checklist for Chapter 14

☑ Only you and your organization can decide if you need an outside consultant.

☑ Crisis management consultants operate much like other outside consultants.

☑ You can, however, expect more 24/7 attention.

☑ Even doing crisis management on your own, you may need a Web consultant.

☑ There are specific questions you should ask any consultant.

☑ Once you've hired a consultant and protected your organization by contract, make them part of your team.

Special Crisis Management Risks

There are exceptions, but in the crisis scenarios I generally describe in this book, the typical catalyst is that something goes wrong or somebody does something wrong, and your crisis response is about addressing and managing that situation. But there are other crises that can arise in which there's no clear evidence you've done anything wrong, or what you've done or are doing is simply a subject of controversy and not "wrong-doing." These sorts of crises can arise when you are "targeted" by a group or individual.

In today's world, three of the main groups such challenges can come from are:

1. The media
2. Activists and bloggers devoted to a cause
3. Governmental agencies or officials

When You're Targeted by the Media

When you're being targeted by the news media it can seem as if the eyes of the world are upon you. It's certainly not good for your blood pressure. In my Crisis Manager online newsletter, I once received an enthusiastic "yes, please" response to my offer to provide some tips on how to minimize the media's attempt to be intrusive.

Okay, I didn't say "intrusive"; I said "how to avoid snooping journalists."

I'm qualified to address this subject not so much because I'm a crisis manager as because I was, formerly, a "snooping journalist" myself, an investigative reporter. In that past life, I felt that any information I could acquire without breaking the law was fair game. I even (gasp) went through trashcans and dumpsters a time or two. I became fairly adept at reading lips, reading body language, and reading papers on your desk upside-down. In other words, I had skills of which most of my "targets" were never aware. Deliberate cultivation of that illusion was part and parcel of what I did.

And I wasn't alone. No doubt historians will record that Woodward and Bernstein (no relation) did a great service to our democracy through their coverage of the Watergate scandal. What historians probably won't record is that they also spawned an entire generation of journalists who believe their most noble pursuit—as well as the clearest path to success—is not just to report the news but to expose crimes, corruption, and generally bad behavior whenever they can and wherever they can find it.

Don't get me wrong. I believe in a free press and that investigative reporting is a good thing. I also believe—in fact, I know—that just because a reporter wants to find a story, that doesn't mean one exists. The problem is, nobody's perfect, and if a reporter digs deep enough with *any* organization they are likely to find *something* that wasn't done right; some dumb decision or misguided policy. So it's wise for organizations to operate under certain guidelines. I call these tips "keeping the media out of the trash."

Keeping the Media Out of the Trash

Here's the first tip: Assume, until proven otherwise, that every reporter is "60 Minutes" slick. Ignore expressions of friendliness. It's highly unlikely a journalist is calling to "catch up" unless you are both actually friends. More likely, they're looking for a story. Let your media training kick into high gear, then proceed confidently.

Here are some others tips:

- Know your loose cannons—most organizations have staff members who tend to say the wrong thing to the wrong person at the wrong time, even if they're well-intentioned and loyal. Many media leads originate with second-hand sources who have heard a loose cannon flapping his or her gums. Make sure such individuals are regularly briefed on and understand your policies on discussing confidential matters with those who have no "need to know."

- Trash is not trash unless it's shredded. When you create draft documents of anything you don't want to see in the media, they should be shredded.

- Have a written policy for every office location about how to handle the media if they just show up, with or without cameras. And rehearse it.

- Warn staff that no matter what they've seen in a TV show, "off the record," "on background," and "not for attribution" are caveats that can be abused or misunderstood by the media and require an educated judgment call to use safely. As a journalist, I would try to get lower-level employees to speak to me and tell them "I won't use your name" when senior management wouldn't give me as much information as I suspected was there. Hence most organizations are better off having a policy that everything said to the media is "on the record" or else you simply don't say it.

Handling an Ambush Interview

It's the nightmare scenario. You're entering or leaving your office—hopefully you have security rules about letting a camera crew actually get into your office without warning. Your mind is somewhere else. The last thing you're expecting is this: the sudden appearance of a microphone or camera in your face.

What do you do? Well, scientists tell us that in situations of surprise or sudden threat, most mammals react based on the "fight or flight" instinct. Not a good idea. First, if you punch a reporter or cameraman, even out of instinct, you might go to jail. Second, likely the camera is rolling, so whatever you do, even running away, will soon be all over the news.

So what do you do? You acknowledge and engage the reporter, but more importantly you take charge of the situation. How? Follow these steps.

1. Stop. Yes, literally stop moving. Do not continue walking while you talk to the reporter. Come to a halt and give them your attention.
2. Don't look defensive. Smile if you can.

SMART   Bᴇ Uɴᴅᴇʀ Cᴏɴᴛʀᴏʟ

An ambush interview is a threat, but it's only a successful threat if you give up control of the situation. Keep your emotions in check and remember *you* control what you do, the reporter

MANAGING   doesn't. You don't have to respond to questions, but you don't want to give them evidence you're avoiding responding. Instead, make it clear you welcome the reporter's questions, you simply need to answer them at another time, and you're happy to set up that *other* time now.

3. Ignoring common courtesies, the reporter probably won't explain why he or she is there. (They'll assume you know you're experiencing an ambush interview.) Instead, they'll hit you with a question.

4. Remember, there is no law that says you have to answer the question. So don't. Instead smile and say that you'd be happy to speak to the reporter, but you can't at the moment. Say you are on your way somewhere and that you're late. Make the "somewhere" you're going totally nonnewsworthy. Examples: "I'm on my way to pick up my daughter from school." (I can pretty much guarantee no TV reporter will deliver such tape to his or her producer.) Or, "I'm late for a meeting" (if they've caught you going into your building).

5. Importantly, though, don't leave it at that. Immediately after you state your excuse for not having time to talk, offer to meet with the reporter later. Preferably the same day. (Make sure to give yourself time to prepare for the interview.)

6. Set up the interview for neutral ground. *Don't* invite the reporter/TV crew into your office (where they can roam the halls filming b-roll to use later).

7. Thank them for their understanding, and the opportunity to speak with them (even if you don't mean it).

8. Prep for the interview. Then go handle it the way you've been media trained.

The benefit of such an approach is that it takes the danger out of the ambush situation. It puts *you* in control of the process (the whole point of the ambush was to take your control of the process away). If you're uncomfortable telling a reporter you don't have time to talk to them when you really do, remember this—you didn't ask to be ambushed.

STAND AND SMILE

TRICKS OF THE TRADE

What if you have an extreme ambush situation? Here's the scenario: You've been ambushed, you explain to the reporter/TV crew that you don't have time to talk but you're happy to set up an interview later. But instead of responding like a normal human being, the reporter simply continues to hurl questions at you (filming all the time, of course). What do you do? Just stand there and smile, regardless of how many questions they throw at you. Don't walk away (they can use that tape to claim you refused to be interviewed). Once you've explained yourself, just stand there and smile. Again, there's no TV news producer on earth who's going to use such meaningless tape on a news broadcast.

When You're Targeted by Activists

As more and more special interest groups become more expert at using the Internet to advance their causes, more and more companies and organizations, and indeed, entire industries, are being targeted by such threats and challenges every year.

Activism The doctrine or practice of vigorous action or involvement as a means of achieving political or other goals, sometimes by demonstrations, protests, etc. **KEY TERM**

While the most visible of these challenges typically take place at the national level, and are obligingly covered by the national media, activism (as a cause of crisis) can manifest itself even down to the local level. (Ask any city council that's tried to build a playground on land the Sierra Club thought should remain "habitat.")

My intention is not to come down on either side of any particular issue, but rather to point out that companies and organizations need to be cognizant of the fact that those who oppose their plans—whoever they are—are likely to be much better today at organizing opposition to those plans than they were even a few years ago.

This dynamic has no particular political bent. The right has learned to use the messaging and organizing power of the Internet as well as the left did before them. Organizations and individuals on both sides of the divide on any particular issue have become or are becoming equally capable of causing a crisis for their opponents. Because *that*, essentially,

SMART

MANAGING

DEALING WITH ACTIVISTS

All activist organizations today have websites. Activist bloggers have blogs. In addition to whatever other media monitoring you do for your organization, follow these simple steps:

1. Investigate which activist organizations and bloggers focus on your industry. You can do this easily by conducting a Google search, a Google blog search, or a number of other search methods.
2. Monitor those that have already demonstrated or may pose a potential threat. Subscribe to their site's RSS feed, or, if they don't offer one, to their online newsletter.
3. Stay on top of these messages. Don't send them to a certain e-mail folder and then forget to look at them for three weeks. Monitor the e-mails regularly; daily is ideal. It may win you several days', or at least a few hours', start on a crisis you weren't anticipating.
4. Don't forget to identify those organizations and bloggers who work in or cover the same industry, but seem more potentially friendly. Establish relationships with these—you may very well need them when a crisis breaks.

is what I'm talking about. Crisis creation. The deliberate creation of a crisis to attain one's personal or organizational goals.

How do you manage such a "purpose driven" crisis? There are several strategies to follow.

1. Don't talk facts, talk values. Activists typically attack their opponents on the basis of values. There's almost always a subtext of morality in whatever they claim. That's fine, but that's only one perspective. Be front and center with your own. Make it an integral part of your key messaging.

2. Use your organization's professional association to build support, but don't stop there. Reach out to others with a possible interest in your situation. That's what your activist opponents are doing. Enlist your contacts and even your stakeholders as allies. Ask them for testimonials, to do interviews, or to spread your messages virally. There are many ways they can help. As with any public argument, the more voices on your side the better.

3. Don't expect, or even try, to control what your allies say with regard to your crisis. Yes, I know I've made strong comments about the need for message control in managing a crisis, but the crises we're

---

Values vs. Facts

Your activist opponent says, "What they want to do is wrong. People will be hurt." And your response is, "Our studies show that ..." Guess who just lost the argument?

Never oppose a "values" statement with a "fact" statement. You will lose your audience, and even those who'll listen to your facts will still think you're a heartless wretch.

Instead, lead with your values. Do you believe what you're doing is the right thing, or don't you? If you do, lead with your chin. You may not convince everyone, but you won't sacrifice the high ground and even those who disagree with you will admire you. And that's the first step in getting them to agree with you.

---

talking about now are different. You aren't looking to speak with one voice, but with many voices. You can't realistically control all the voices you need to arouse, and even if you could, everyone speaking from the same script would sound, at best, orchestrated, and, at worst, worse. Provide your allies with your key messages and let them take it from there.

Last, don't rely on your national trade association to fight your battle for you. Very likely they've faced this sort of challenge themselves, or one of their members has, and they can often provide advice, recommendations, strategies, and tools to help you through your crisis. But remember, their mission is to the industry as a whole, not to defend you individually. Take their help, but don't take direction.

When You're Targeted by an Official Investigation

A full explanation of how to manage the crisis of being targeted by an official governmental investigation is outside the scope of this book. If your organization is facing one of these challenges—where your CEO or a member of senior management could actually end up in jail—I strongly recommend you hire an outside crisis management consultant (as well as expert legal representation). But I still think it's important to address this subject briefly, so you can get a sense of how such challenges are dealt with. You'll see many commonalities with the other types of crises we talk about in this book.

"Officialdom" in the United States is made up of a number of levels, everything from your county district attorney to your state attorney general to the U.S. Justice Department. And those are only the law enforcement offices. There are also county and state commissions, county and state regulatory agencies, "special districts" that oversee issues on a multicounty basis, and of course, federal regulatory agencies. There are only several hundred of those.

And all of them are public agencies. They variously have the authority to fine, indict, or simply issue findings that can damage your organization's reputation. And since the implication is that these entities work for the benefit of the public, the media typically stand ready and willing to cover their findings and announcements without subjecting them to much scrutiny.

And then, of course, there's Congress. Which has the authority to call you on the carpet over whatever they want to investigate this month. Not that anyone in Congress ever stoops to such things for political purposes, of course.

How do you cope? There are several strategies in managing an official investigation.

- Practice transparency. Provide access. Cooperate with official (not necessarily media) interview requests. Of course you understand there are questions, and you're looking forward to answering them.
- Put forth a public image of confidence. No matter how innocent you are, if you act guilty, you will *look* guilty. And in the crisis management business, all too often perception trumps reality.
- Make it clear—especially to the media—that you are cooperating with officials and want to solve the problem.
- While all this is going on, consider the pros and cons of going on the offensive—if such an opportunity exists. Let's face it; we all know there are times when a public official's motives for launching an investigation are not noble. There *may* be an opportunity to turn the table on your accuser. But you have to tread very carefully here. And you'd better have excellent media contacts.

Manager's Checklist for Chapter 15

☑ Not all crises arise out of wrongdoing.

☑ The media, activist opponents, government, and others can all be sources of unexpected crises.

☑ Handle all media requests carefully. Don't assume because they act friendly they are friendly.

☑ To manage a crisis created by activists, use their own strategies and methods against them.

☑ In official investigations, it's sometimes possible to play offense and not just defense. Just be very careful.

Moral Imperatives and the Future of Crisis Management

A deranged young man shows up at a supermarket parking lot where the local congressperson is meeting with constituents. He pulls a gun and begins shooting. Almost everyone scatters, running for their lives. But not everyone. As the gunman reloads, a man jumps up and grabs him. Then another. As they wrestle with the gunman, an elderly lady nearby grabs the new clip of ammo he's trying to load into his semi-automatic pistol. Without it, the gunman no longer dominates the scene, and is held until the police can arrive.

Fortunately, 99 percent of the crises we describe in this book do not entail such tragic circumstances. But I bring up this incident to make a point about crisis management that informs the entire process—a crisis brings out the best and worst in people.

When terrorists killed thousands of Americans on September 11, the crisis communications response of companies and organizations across the country demonstrated that some were well prepared, but most were not. That most had been, as suspected, complacent.

The most directly affected companies, such as the hijacked airlines, followed most of the important tenets of crisis communications. And a small number of adequately prepared online retailers and other service providers notified their customers, expressing their regret that they couldn't ship orders as usual and what they planned to do about it. Their consideration in contacting their stakeholders no doubt scored a lot of "PR points" (I know, I was one of those customers). On the other hand, there were a lot of obviously unprepared organizations from which customers never heard.

Some businesses—PRNewswire comes to mind—offered their services free to those most directly affected by the tragedy. A marvelous, humanitarian response—and damned good PR.

But then, of course, there were the exploiters; the ones offering us 10 percent off on survival gear, American flags—or guns. Maybe they sold more and made money in the short run, but at what cost? This isn't meant as a judgment on anyone's character. It is meant as an advisory of what you can expect when you or your organization face a meaningful crisis.

Many years ago, a colleague of mine worked with a small, privately owned seed and garden supply company that had just purchased an entire railway tanker car full of a popular insecticide. It was a big purchase for a small company, but they knew the product would sell. Gardeners loved it. What the company didn't know was that the EPA was about to rule the product a carcinogen. Once that news broke, the company was flooded with calls both from the media and the retailers it served.

The media wanted to know the company's intentions. Were they going to distribute the product to lawn and garden centers despite the EPA ban? The garden centers were, EPA ban aside, asking for just that. They wanted the product because *their* customers were clamoring for it, knowing it would soon be unavailable.

The owner of the company had a ready answer. They would not distribute the product, and would absorb the cost of buying it from the manufacturer. In making his announcement, the owner simply said, "This company helps people grow flowers and vegetables. We don't sell things that cause cancer."

His decision was a major hit to the company's bottom line (and his own personal pocket), but the goodwill generated by his decision paid dividends in positive PR and customer loyalty for years after that. Who doesn't want to do business with a company that values public health over personal profit, and is willing to match their values with their own wallet? Unfortunately, such benefits are impossible to calculate.

Not all organizational leaders have such a clear moral compass to help them deal with a crisis. Often, when a company or someone working for the company has done something wrong, intentionally or not, the knee-jerk reaction is denial, or the "ostrich effect" I've described, or an eagerness to shunt the blame onto someone else. Or just the minimal action required by law or governmental regulation.

But organizational lapses or errors must be met with positive corrective action, and that action must be communicated to stakeholders. If it's not, the public can be very unforgiving.

At the same time, the public can be very forgiving—*if* the organization's actions and communications during a crisis are consistent with the Five Tenets. (And yes, I am listing them again, because they are *that* important.)

1. Prompt
2. Compassionate
3. Honest
4. Informative
5. Interactive

Reading them again, you'll notice that they all either contain or imply a moral component. This is because in a crisis the public expects organizations to do what's right, not just what's required. Companies like Bridgestone/Firestone, Merck, BP, Toyota, and many more, have learned that lesson the painful way.

KEEP AHEAD OF THE CURVE

TRICKS OF THE TRADE

Crisis management is mainly about averting a crisis. But when one breaks, it's about responding to it in a way that will minimize organizational damage. Crisis managers *must* keep up with the recent advances in communications technologies. But while the vehicles of communications may change, the principles remain the same. Be prompt, compassionate, honest, informative, and give stakeholders a voice. Do that, and regardless what new technology they come up with tomorrow, you'll be ahead of the curve.

The Future of Crisis Management

I believe that the diversity of and dependence on technology has and will continue to create the potential for more and different kinds of crises. Since most organizations will continue to engage in insufficient crisis preparedness, there will be, quite simply, more crises that interrupt business, damage reputation, or both—with consequent impact on the bottom line.

However, some of that same technology will allow crisis managers to respond faster, more efficiently, and with instant worldwide impact. It will allow them to virtually project themselves anywhere in the world, adding some real effect and nonverbal communications to long-distance contact.

But while the technology will change, the principles remain the same.

SMART MANAGING

COMMUNICATE—OR ELSE

Whatever your comfort level with the rapid evolution of communications technology, as a crisis manager you can't afford to be "behind the curve." Organizations that were slow to adapt to now-familiar things, like personal computers, or the Internet and e-mail, greatly increased their vulnerability to a crisis until they caught up. We've seen the same thing in just the past few years with Twitter. The fact is, the public is embracing new technologies and means of communication as quickly as they can be invented or developed. Your stakeholders are out there communicating. You better be there, too.

I was once asked in an interview if I were scripting a film that takes place in the future in which a crisis manager hero has to confront an organizational crisis of global proportions, what would it look like?

I said it would involve views of crisis team members worldwide and in Earth orbit virtually conferencing, drafting documents, and giving orders from their mobile computing and communications devices. Shots of at least one "vital to the crisis" system going down and a fully automated replacement system on another continent immediately going online.

Of course, in the "some things never change" category, there would also be footage of at least one senior executive or attorney saying that no public statement was really needed and the organization should just "wait and see" what happened.

But in the end, our crisis manager hero and his or her team would manage the crisis. The organization would survive, and in fact, see its reputation and the loyalty of its stakeholders enhanced as a result of its forthright and expeditious Crisis Management. Roll credits.

Where Do You Fit In?

While an organization's crisis management strategy must be endorsed and supported by senior management, the impetus for developing such a strategy doesn't have to start at the top.

Let's say you're the PR chief for a mid-sized corporation in high tech. You know there's a long list of things that could go wrong. If and when they do, you know that you're the one who's going to have to explain them. Your CEO is all in favor of crisis preparedness and says, "Sure, let's do it." What's your first step? And your second? And your third? Assuming you've already identified an expert on crisis preparedness, either on staff or a consultant, the primary steps he or she should help you take are:

1. Conduct a vulnerability audit.
2. Engage in crisis planning, including the development of key messaging for each contingency.
3. Conduct crisis response training and simulations.
4. Rinse. Repeat. As our guys and gals in the military will tell you, training without repetition isn't training.

Manager's Checklist for Chapter 16

☑ Expect a crisis to bring out the best and worst in people.

☑ You can be an agent of change in your business or organization by championing crisis preparedness.

☑ Technology is increasing the likelihood of organizations suffering a crisis, but it's also enhancing the tools crisis managers can use to respond.

☑ Hope for the best. Prepare for the worst.

Index

About the Author

Jonathan L. Bernstein, president of Bernstein Crisis Management, Inc. has more than 25 years of experience meeting clients' needs in all aspects of crisis management—crisis response, vulnerability assessment, planning, training, and simulations. Prior to launching what was then known as Bernstein Communications in 1994, Bernstein created and served as the first director of the Crisis Communications Group for Ruder Finn, Inc., one of the world's largest public relations agencies.

Bernstein's crisis and issues management experience has encompassed a wide range of industries and subjects, to include accounting, architecture, associations, banking, charities, education, environment, financial services, food (retail and B2B), health care, housing, insurance, labor & employment, litigation, manufacturing, product recalls, professional services, real estate development, religious institutions, securities, security, senior housing, and white-collar crime. He is a self-admitted "geek," online since 1982, who has pioneered strategies and tactics for Internet-centered crisis management.

His past experience includes corporate, agency, and nonprofit public relations positions, preceded by five years of investigative and feature journalism — to include a stint with investigative reporter/columnist Jack Anderson. He is a veteran of five years in U.S. Army Military Intelligence covert operations.

Bernstein is publisher and editor of Crisis Manager, a first-of-its-kind e-mail newsletter written for "those who are crisis managers whether they want to be or not," currently read in 75 countries, and a blogger at the popular Huffington Post site. His commercially published *Keeping the Wolves at Bay: Media Training* has been described as "an outstanding foundation for preparing individuals and organizations for effective crisis management." Bernstein has been quoted as an expert source by a wide range of media outlets, to include AP, ABC News, BBC, Bloomberg News, Business 2.0, *BusinessWeek*, CBS, CNBC, ESPN, Forbes, Fox News, *Inc.* magazine, NPR, Reuters, *The Christian Science Monitor*, TheStreet.com, *The Wall Street Journal*, TIME magazine, *USA Today*, and many local and regional publications. A *PR Week* feature story entitled

"The Crunch-Time Counselors" identified Bernstein as one of 22 "people who should be on the speed dial in a crisis."

A popular speaker at a wide variety of industry functions, Bernstein has been featured and praised for presentations and workshops at events such as the American Bar Association, Arizona Bar Association, Association of Corporate Counsel, National Summit on Campus Security, World Conference on Disaster Management, National Symposium for Healthcare Executives, Builder 100 Conference, International Facility Management Association, the National School Boards Association, and Intel Corporation's Worldwide Issue Prevention & Management Group,

A married father of five, Bernstein is a yoga practitioner, 1960s-style folksinger, and is very active in community service. Visit his website at www.bernsteincrisismanagement.com.

CPSIA information can be obtained at www.ICGtesting.com
Printed in the USA
BVOW01s1434150315

391669BV00008B/66/P